THE HOPI-TEWA

BY

EDWARD P. DOZIER

UNIVERSITY OF CALIFORNIA PRESS

BERKELEY AND LOS ANGELES

1954

University of California Publications in American Archaeology and Ethnology

Editors (Los Angeles): R. L. Beals, G. W. Brainerd, W. R. Goldschmidt

Volume 44, No. 3, pp. 259–376, 4 figures in text, 4 maps

Submitted by editors September 23, 1953

Issued October 29, 1954

Price, $1.50

University of California Press

Berkeley and Los Angeles

California

◇

Cambridge University Press

London, England

ACKNOWLEDGMENTS

THE FIELD WORK for this study was financed by a predoctoral fellowship from the Social Science Research Council and a John Hay Whitney Foundation fellowship. A postdoctoral grant from the Wenner-Gren Foundation for Anthropological Research made possible the preparation of this monograph for publication. To all these foundations I wish to express my thanks and appreciation.

The initial field study was made under the sponsorship of the Department of Anthropology and Sociology of the University of California at Los Angeles. I am particularly grateful to Dr. Ralph Beals, Dr. Walter Goldschmidt, and Dr. Harry Hoijer of that department for constant aid and advice in the course of my field work and the preparation of this manuscript.

I am indebted to a number of institutions for the services extended to me in the course of my field research and the work on this manuscript. The personnel in the Departments of Anthropology at the University of Arizona, New Mexico, and Oregon generously made available their help and facilities. The Museum of Northern Arizona, at Flagstaff, was extremely helpful, and I am happy to extend my appreciation to its staff. Dr. Harold S. Colton of that museum generously made available his excellent personal library on the Southwest for my research. My grateful thanks are communicated to him.

In particular, for encouragement and for many suggestions, I wish to express my thanks to Drs. Florence Hawley Ellis, W. W. Hill, and Leslie Spier of the Department of Anthropology, University of New Mexico.

Dr. Fred Eggan placed at my disposal in the beginning of my research a copy of his then unpublished chapter on "Hano Social Organization," which proved to be exceedingly helpful. For this and other information he supplied from time to time in the course of my study I wish to express my sincere appreciation.

For their reading of the whole or parts of the manuscript and for offering many fruitful suggestions I am thankful to Dr. and Mrs. John Adair, Cornell University; Mr. and Mrs. Robert Agger, University of Oregon; Dr. George Barker, University of California, Los Angeles; Mr. and Mrs. John Connelley, Shongopovi Day School, Hopi Reservation; Mr. Oliver La Farge, president of the Association on American Indian Affairs; Mr. Robert Sheward, University of Arizona; Mr. Watson Smith, Peabody Museum, Harvard University; and Dr. and Mrs. Edward H. Spicer, University of Arizona.

For help with charts and drawings I am indebted to Mr. Thomas Bahti, Desert House, Tucson, Arizona, and Mr. Milton Snow, Navaho Field Service, Window Rock, Arizona.

I also deeply appreciate the assistance given by my wife, Marianne Fink Dozier, in the field work and in typing and copyreading my manuscript.

Finally, but not least in importance, I wish to express my thanks and appreciation to my many Hopi and Hopi-Tewa friends without whom this study could not, of course, have been made. To one family in particular, who I am sure would prefer to be unnamed, I wish to express my thanks. This family provided a home and a host of relatives whom I am honored in the Hopi-Tewa manner to claim as my own.

CONTENTS

TABLES

FIGURES

MAPS

INTRODUCTION

TEWA VILLAGE,[1] the Tewa-speaking community in northern Arizona, is the eastern-most pueblo on the Hopi Reservation. It is one of three pueblos on First Mesa; the other two communities are Shoshonean Hopi in speech and culture. Although the inhabitants of Tewa Village speak another language and are set off culturally from the Hopi people, nothing about the outward appearance of the pueblo suggests this separatist quality. Tewa Village, in village plan, in architectural features of the houses, and in dress and material possessions of its inhabitants, appears to be a typical Hopi pueblo. Even in the physical appearance of the Hopi-Tewa no difference between them and the Hopi is apparent. Both belong to a fairly homogenous puebloid physical type. Culturally, however, the two peoples are quite distinct. The analysis of their differences is the main concern of this study.

Although abundant literature exists on the Hopi, there is very little information regarding the Hopi-Tewa. Since Tewa Village is a comparatively recent community and its culture is manifestly different from that of the Hopi, those interested in the more colorful and ceremonially richer Hopi culture have by-passed it. The Hopi-Tewa, however, are an important group in themselves, and a study of them is needed. Moreover, they represent a group in which studies of social and cultural change promise fruitful returns. Freire-Marreco (1914) and Parsons (1936a, pp. xliv–xlv) realized the importance of such a study of the Hopi-Tewa, and recently Eggan (1950, p. 175) has reaffirmed this importance. Virtually all that we know of the Hopi-Tewa comes from fragmentary accounts made by investigators preoccupied with a study of the Shoshonean-speaking Hopi. Eggan has summarized this information in exemplary fashion in his recent book (1950, pp. 139–175) and has raised many problems for further investigation.

This study investigates some of the problems of the Hopi-Tewa. It is first of all a study of the distinctive elements of their culture. It is concerned with the history of these people, and particularly with the social mechanism by which they have preserved their identity during three centuries of close association not only with the Hopi on First Mesa but also with the Spanish and the Anglo-Americans.

The ancestors of the Hopi-Tewa can be traced with assurance over a period of 650 years. Struggles against nomadic tribes, droughts, smallpox epidemics, and Spanish oppression characterized the history of the group before they left their homeland in New Mexico and settled with the Hopi more than 250 years ago. The Hopi-Tewa were a refugee group escaping from Spanish oppression. Legends, myths, and information supplied by Hopi and Hopi-Tewa informants also indicate that they were in a minority status at Hopi for a very long time. In this new home-land they clung tenaciously to their own cultural forms and effectively resisted acculturation with their neighbors. It is interesting, however, to note that, although pronounced differences still exist between the two groups, resistance to acculturation has declined sharply since the beginning of the century. At the present time it appears that the two groups are actually merging and that the antagonisms have for

[1] The terms "Hopi-Tewa" for the people and "Tewa Village" for their pueblo will be used in this study. Although the ancestors of the residents of Tewa Village were very probably Tano, the present-day inhabitants resent being identified as such (see "Early History and Culture," in chap. i).

[259]

the most part subsided.[2] The change took place coincident with accelerated American activities, such as the establishment of the agency and of government schools, the dissemination of stock-raising information, trading-post activities, the employment of Indians for wage work, and the influx of tourists.

An important result of American contact has been the reorientation of the value system on First Mesa—a reorientation more compatible with Hopi-Tewa values. There is abundant evidence that the Hopi-Tewa demonstrated very early in the American period a willingness to coöperate with Americans and to participate in American activities. The personality of the Hopi-Tewa proved congenial to Americans, and the Indians adjusted remarkably well to the changing situation brought about by American contact. The success of the Hopi-Tewa in American activities seems to have resulted in reduced tensions on First Mesa and in emulation of the Hopi-Tewa by their Hopi neighbors. This in turn paved the way for greater interdependence and coöperation among the three villages on First Mesa. As a consequence, the minority status of the Hopi-Tewa began to dissolve and the present trend toward an integrated First Mesa society commenced.

It should be emphasized, however, that participation of Hopi-Tewa and First Mesa Hopi in the American cultural system is primarily in the economic realm, and even here the fruits of the activity are being handled largely in terms of the traditional pattern. Basic American institutions and concepts have had little effect on either the Hopi-Tewa or their neighbors. Thus, the individual-profit motive and Christianity seem to have made little impression on these people. The distribution and consumption of food and goods operate within the kinship system and in the units of extended family, clan, and linked clan. The systems of belief and ritual also have native roots.

The integrative process on First Mesa is also evident in ceremonial life. Hopi-Tewa ceremonial activity is decreasing, whereas Hopi religious ritual is still vigorous and complex. The Hopi-Tewa, in relinquishing their own ceremonies, are moving into the rich Hopi ceremonial life.

What the future will hold is difficult to predict. The pressure of the system of values and the institutions of white Americans may be too strong. Certainly, government activity, schools, and off-reservation employment will continue to exert pressure. Yet the conservative nature of Hopi and Hopi-Tewa culture makes it likely that the kind of integration First Mesa society has achieved will endure for a long time.

FIELD PROCEDURE

In June, 1949, I visited First Mesa for a preliminary survey of the Hopi-Tewa. As a native Tewa-speaking member of Santa Clara Pueblo, a village of the Rio Grande Tewa in New Mexico, I was received with considerable warmth—as any other visitor from my village would have been. Only after several weeks did I make known my desire to study, and even then I mentioned only the language.

The following fall, I rented part of a house in Polacca at the foot of First Mesa,[3] which gave me the privacy and detachment I desired and still permitted me to spend a great deal of time on top of the mesa.

---

[2] The history of this resistance was not fully realized when a preliminary paper on the Hopi-Tewa was published (see Dozier, 1951, pp. 56–65). Although the article is still valid in the analysis of the resistance patterns, the implication that these patterns are as strong today as they were in the past is incorrect.

[3] See chap. ii, below, for maps and descriptions of First Mesa communities.

My relationships in the community were intimate; whenever I left I found upon my return that I was warmly welcomed. On trips to Flagstaff, Gallup, Albuquerque, and occasionally to my home in Santa Clara, I often took Tewa villagers with me. Once I brought back a family of Santa Clara Tewa to participate in the *Yandewa* ceremony which has been borrowed from Santa Clara Pueblo. The Santa Clara family and I were feted in almost every Hopi-Tewa home. This provided an opportunity for observing the differences in general behavior between the two groups and the relation between them; for example, the deep respect the Hopi-Tewa have for their linguistic kinfolk. The visit was useful in cementing my own relations with the Hopi-Tewa, for I came to be regarded as a very close friend, and everyone began to exchange clan relationship terms with me.

Most informants volunteered to help; I did not need to ask their assistance. A great deal of the information was obtained through conversations in the Tewa language; the use of this language put my informants at ease, and thus the atmosphere was rarely artificial. Many came as visitors to pass the time of day; indeed, they were more my friends than my informants. They came because they were "lonely" and wanted to spend a day or evening away from home, to discuss affairs close to themselves, or to talk idly about events in the outside world. I rarely urged or directed conversation; the visitors chose their own topics, with only subtle guidance toward items of special interest to me.

Eventually about half a dozen became more intimate and proved to be excellent informants. When their complete confidence and interest had been gained, I could discuss the true nature of the study and get meticulous information by taking notes in front of them.

In the summer of 1950, under another grant, I returned to Tewa Village with my bride—a Caucasian girl. I feared that I might not be received as warmly in my new role. However, when the Hopi-Tewa addressed my wife with the appropriate relationship term for a woman married to a man of one's own clan, my anxiety abated. My wife and I resided in Polacca during the fall and winter of 1950–51. Like the Hopi and Hopi-Tewa, we kept an "open house."

ORTHOGRAPHY

The phonetic symbols used in this monograph are described briefly below. The extent to which Hopi-Tewa sounds differ from those of the Rio Grande Tewa[4] has not yet been determined. Some of the differences will appear in this list (cf. Santa Clara phonemes in Hoijer and Dozier, 1949). A detailed description of Hopi-Tewa sounds and a comparison with Santa Clara Tewa is under preparation.

Vowels:		*Oral*		*Nasal*	
		short	*long*	*short*	*long*
High front unrounded		ı	ı·	ị	..
Mid front unrounded		e	e·	..	..
Higher-lower front unrounded		ε	ε·	ε̣	ε̣·
Low front unrounded		a	a·	ą	ą·
High back rounded		u	u·	ų	ų·
Mid back rounded		o	o·	..	..

4 For a description of Tewa phonemes, see Hoijer and Dozier, 1949, pp. 139–144.

Diphthongs:

e^i
a^i
a^u

Stops:	*Voiced*	*Voiceless*	*Glottalized*
Bilabial.. .	b	p	p'
Apical-alveolar.	d	t	t'
Flapped	r		
Dorsal-mid-velar	g	k	k'
Labialized...	..	k^w	k'^{w}
Palatalized .	ɢ .	k^y	k'^{y}
Glottal. .	ʔ		

Affricates	*Voiceless*	*Glottalized*
Alveolar... .	c	c'
Blade-alveolar..	č	

Nasal continuants:	*Voiced*
Bilabial..	m
Alveolar...	n
Palatalized.	n^y
Velar... .	ŋ

Lateral	*Voiced*
Alveolar...	l

Spirants:	*Voiced*	*Voiceless*	*Frictionless*
Bilabial...	v	f	w
Interdental...	..	θ	..
Alveolar...	..	s	..
Palatal.. .	..	š	y
Velar.....	..	x	..
Labiovelar. ..	..	x^w	..
Glottal ...	..	..	h
Labialized glottal. .	..	..	h^w

Stress and pitch accent:

High	á
Middle	(unmarked)
Low	à
Falling	â

CHAPTER I

HISTORICAL BACKGROUND

ACCORDING TO recent archaeological reports, the ancestors of the Hopi-Tewa appeared on the archaeological horizon as early as 650 years ago.[1] At this time the forebears of the Hopi-Tewa were abandoning the Mesa Verde area and migrating southward. By 1350 they were established in the Galisteo basin in New Mexico. Their neighbors to the north and south were linguistically related Tanoan peoples; but from the west, the Keres, another puebloid people, culturally and linguistically different from the Tanoans, were coming into the Rio Grande area. To the east were nomadic tribes, probably Apachean-speaking, who raided the ancestors of the Hopi-Tewa and periodically, while on friendly terms, traded with them. In 1540 Francisco Vásquez de Coronado and his party entered the Galisteo basin. Then followed several more or less important *entradas* in rapid succession, and in 1598 the actual colonization of New Mexico began. For one hundred years the Galisteo basin peoples experienced the Christianizing and civilizing efforts of the Spanish religious and civil authorities; but finally, in 1696, they fled to Hopi, and there they have lived, relatively undisturbed by whites until quite recently.

EARLY HISTORY AND CULTURE

Historical evidence indicates quite clearly that the Hopi-Tewa were actually Thano. or Tano, and not Tewa (Reed, 1943a, p. 73).[2] The Tano, who are also known in the anthropological literature as Southern Tewa, formerly occupied the Galisteo basin south of Santa Fe. The Tewa proper, however, lived north of Santa Fe in the Española valley. From historical accounts, as well as ethnologic data, we are aware that there was little difference linguistically between the Tano and the Tewa (J. M. Espinosa, 1940, pp. 76 and 80). The similarities in social organization noted between the present Hopi-Tewa and the Rio Grande Tewa in this study also make it likely that there were only minor differences in other cultural features. In a tribal or political sense, however, the Tano were quite distinct and were treated separately from the Tewa by early Spanish authorities (Reed, 1943b, p. 254).

Identification as Tewa seems to be a recent desire of the Hopi-Tewa. Very old men and women at Tewa Village speak of themselves as θá·nu Téwah (Thano Tewa), but the majority of the present-day inhabitants insist on calling themselves Tewa and their pueblo Tewa Village. Increasing contacts in late years with the Rio Grande Tewa no doubt have brought about this change. The Hopi-Tewa had much prestige to gain from such an affiliation, which was facilitated by the ability of both groups to understand each other.[3]

After the Pueblo Indian revolt of 1680–1692, the Tano tribe was dispersed; however, for a brief period, some of the Tano moved to the Santa Cruz valley, north of Santa Fe. Troubles with the Spaniards persisted, and about 1696 this group, the ancestors of the present Hopi-Tewa, migrated to Hopi.

[1] Reed (1952, pp. 11–18) reports that the history of the ancestors of the Hopi-Tewa can be traced with reasonable assurance over a period of 1,500 years.
[2] See also Dozier, 1951, pp. 56 and 57. It is very probable that some Northern Tewa also accompanied the original migrants, but historical and ethnologic data indicate that the main group were Tano.
[3] For another discussion of this situation, see Dozier, 1951, p. 62.

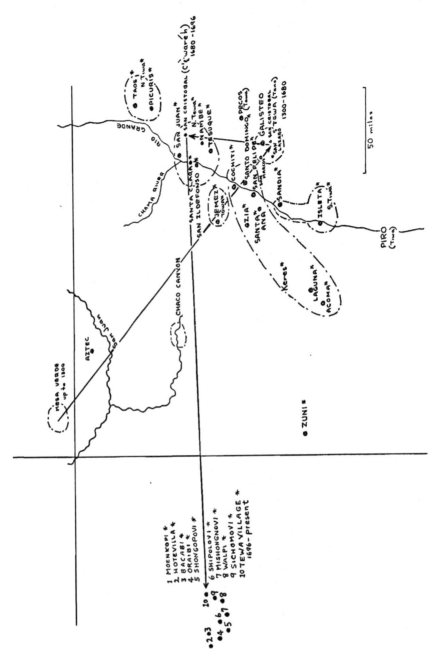

Map 1. Distribution of the pueblos: late prehistoric, early historic, and present-day. Present linguistic groups and pueblos are marked with an asterisk.

Although the Tanoan-speaking[4] peoples were found by early Spanish explorers in the region in which they lived in later historic times, archaeological evidence indicates that they had moved into the area from the north. According to some recently developed hypotheses, these tribes came into the northern Rio Grande region from the San Juan archaeological area; that is, primarily from Mesa Verde and Chaco.[5] For example, Erik Reed (1949, p. 182) reports:

> The basic culture and population of the Rio Grande was and is, in this hypothesis, Tanoan Anasazi.[6] In early periods, the whole Rio Grande area may have been Tiwa-speaking; and the Jemez people, extending eastward across to Pecos, may have come in from the Chaco region, toward the close of the Chaco period of the San Juan [twelfth century]. Upon final abandonment of the San Juan, about 1300, people of the Mesa Verde phase, very possibly Tewas,[7] moved into the region around Santa Fe.

Later, Reed (1950, p. 133) modifies this hypothesis by deriving the Towa from the prehistoric Largo culture of the Gallina area, and the Tewa from both Chaco and Mesa Verde, and assuming that the Southern Tewa, or Tano, came in last, in 1300.

Reed (1949, pp. 168–169) advances this hypothesis from the correlation of a number of important San Juan Anasazi archaeological features with those of the northern Rio Grande Tanoan region. Particularly strong evidence that the Galisteo basin area was peopled from the Mesa Verde area is afforded by the pottery. About 1300, at the time of the abandonment of the San Juan archaeological region, the characteristic Mesa Verde black-on-white pottery suddenly appeared in large quantities in the Galisteo basin and adjacent districts.

In terms of nonmaterial culture, Florence Hawley Ellis (1951, p. 149) has suggested an outline of prehistoric Tanoan social organization which seems plausible. She suggests that the Tanoans developed "a working structure based on the united bilateral family group, the larger parallel group of bilateral relatives, and the still larger dual division usually referred to as the 'moiety,' with its tendency toward endogamy."

I would add to these traits the important moiety societies, which are very strong among the Tewa. These societies, though curative, have important governmental functions as well. There are two caciques in a village—one from each moiety—who alternate seasonally in governing the pueblo: the Winter Chief is in charge from the autumnal equinox to the spring equinox; the Summer Chief governs the pueblo

---

[4] The term *Tanoan* designates the linguistically affiliated though mutually unintelligible language groups of Tewa (Santa Clara, San Ildefonso, San Juan, Tesuque, Nambe, Tewa Village [Tano]); Towa (Jemez and, until 1838, the pueblo of Pecos); and Tiwa (Taos, Picuris, Sandia, Isleta). A number of villages, now extinct, south of the Tiwa district were known to the Spaniards as the Piro pueblos. The Piro language was merely a dialect of the Tiwa; its position appears to be similar to that of Tano with respect to Tewa. (Hodge, 1912, Pt. 2, p. 687; Hoijer, 1946, pp. 22–23.) See map 1.

[5] See especially Reed, 1949, pp. 163–184; Ellis, 1951, pp. 148–151; Eggan, 1950, pp. 304–321. Florence Hawley Ellis suggests that all Tanoans came from the San Juan drainage area, and that the original occupants of Chaco were possibly Zunis but more probably Keres. She bases her suggestion on the close pottery and kiva affiliation between Chaco and the Zuni-Acoma-Cebolleta area near Mount Taylor, which she considers ancestral to the western pueblos of historic times. She proposes that after the initial abandonment of Chaco, parts of the sites were temporarily occupied possibly by "Southern Tewa" peoples working southeastward toward the middle Rio Grande later in the twelfth or early in the thirteenth century. (Ellis, 1951, p. 149.)

[6] Anasazi is a broad division of prehistoric culture, found in the four-corners area of Utah, Colorado, New Mexico, and Arizona, with local divisions or stems, such as Kayenta, Mesa Verde, Aztec, Chaco, and Largo.

[7] It is likely that at this early date the Tewa and Tano were not differentiated into two groups.

the rest of the year. Members in each society are recruited by vow, by trespass, or by being cured of a serious illness. A cacique has a right- and a left-"arm" assistant. When a cacique dies, his right-arm assistant succeeds him, the left-arm assistant moves to the position of right-arm assistant, and another man is selected from the society—seniority is the basis for the selection—to be left-arm assistant.

The Tewa moiety societies seem to be homologous to the "kiva societies" of Taos (organized within each moiety). These societies may have had separate "houses" in the prehistoric past, and this may be the explanation of the several small kivas to a village, in the ruins of the Mesa Verde area.[8] The Taos "kiva societies" and the Tewa moiety societies have no clan characteristics. It is possible that the Mesa Verde kivas were the meeting and retreat houses of such societies and were not clan kivas.[9]

The Tano in the Galisteo basin in the fourteenth century probably had the characteristics listed above. Culturally there may have been no distinction between them and the Tewa, whose territory joined theirs on the north. Indeed, they may have been one people at this early period. The Tiwa and Towa peoples who preceded the Tewa-speaking peoples into the Rio Grande region, in terms of Reed's hypothesis, may have exhibited some differences. Yet linguistically (Whorf and Trager, 1937, pp. 609–624) the Tewa, Tiwa, and Towa are related; and since Reed and other archaeologists agree that the Tiwa and Towa also came from the San Juan region and have basic Anasazi traits, the cultural differences may have been slight.

Influences from nomadic tribes may have been more important. The Tano lived on the eastern frontier of the pueblo country. Castañeda in 1541 reported that sixteen years previously the Teya, perhaps an Apache tribe, had devastated the area (Hodge, 1907, pp. 356–357). There were probably also periods of friendliness with these tribes. Castañeda (*loc. cit.*) also reports friendly relations between the people of Pecos and the Teya:

"These people [the Teya] knew the people in the settlements and were friendly with them, and they went there to spend the winter under the wings of the settlements. The inhabitants did not dare to let them come inside, because they cannot trust them. Although they are received as friends, and trade with them, they do not stay in the villages over night, but outside under the wings."

Such peaceful relations are favorable conditions for the exchange and borrowing of cultural elements. It is difficult to determine, however, what specific institutions were borrowed. Perhaps war societies—such as the man's war society and the woman's scalp society of the Rio Grande Tewa—were borrowed or their development was inspired by other tribes. Personality traits and the more aggressive and individualistic nature of the Tanoans in general were also perhaps developed as a result of this relationship. The Tano's "warrior-like qualities," according to tradition, prompted the Hopi to invite the Tano "to come and settle at First Mesa and be our protectors."[10]

The major cultural influence came, however, from a new migrant group, apparently from the west. This influence is first evident archaeologically in the form of a

---

[8] Meetings and retreats of moiety societies are held in the homes of the society leaders and not in the kivas (my ethnographic notes on Rio Grande Tewa pueblos).

[9] Parsons, 1936, discusses the kiva societies of Taos. Information on Tewa societies is from my notes on Rio Grande Tewa pueblos.

[10] Notes from First Mesa Hopi informants.

new glaze-paint redware. That this ware was neither imported nor made by local imitation of an imported ware is suggested by its sudden appearance in large quantities and by the excellence of its manufacture. Reed (1949, p. 171) summarizes the significance of this change: "The abruptness of the change to glaze-paint redware, which is of the best quality from the first, and the fact that other new traits make their appearance at the same time suggests actual immigration of a new group to the upper Rio Grande in the first half of the fourteenth century."

According to Reed (1950, p. 134), before the introduction of the glaze-paint ware the upper Rio Grande Tanoan archaeological region was characterized by the following diagnostic features: black-on-white and gray corrugated pottery, full-grooved axes, circular kivas, and lambdoid cranial deformation. About the middle of the fourteenth century, with the appearance of glaze-paint redware and presumably with the entrance of a new people into the area, a set of new traits appeared: rectangular kivas, a ¾-grooved polished axe, and vertical-occipital cranial deformation. About this culture, Reed (1949, p. 182) reports: "This culture seems to have developed in east-central Arizona and to have spread thence, 650 years ago, into Hohokam, Hopi and Zuni areas. Western cultural features reached the Rio Grande, in somewhat attenuated form, shortly before 1350, probably brought by actual immigrants, perhaps the Keresans."[11]

Reed correlates the first set of traits with patrilineal moieties, nonhereditary kiva groups, and perhaps with male ownership of houses. The second set of traits he correlates with clans, masks, the katcina cult, medicine societies, female descent, and female house ownership.

Reed's correlation has been suggested, of course, by the dichotomy between western and eastern historic pueblos pointed out by ethnologists (Parsons, 1939; Hawley, 1937, p. 504). The western pueblos—Hopi and Zuni, at least—have several kivas to a village; in these pueblos the emphasis is on clan, female ownership of houses and garden plots, matrilocal residence, and the katcina cult. Major religious emphasis is on weather control—rain production to make crops grow. The eastern Tanoan pueblos have one or two kivas to a village; in these pueblos patrilineal moieties, bilateral families with patrilineal tendencies, and male ownership of houses are stressed; the katcina cult and clan are less important and in some cases are absent. The major religious orientation revolves around the moieties and curing.[12] The Rio Grande Keres are intermediate. Hawley (1950b, p. 511) characterizes the Keres as follows:

We might hazard the hypothesis that in general the Keresans appear to have clanship as a native trait, originally of importance in government, religion, and marriage control and that the patrilineal concept for membership in "moiety" was superimposed on their own dual kiva-kachina system. More important to the majority of Keresans at present than either are their "medicine societies," whose duties cover not only curing, but also weather control and selection of religious

---

[11] The Keres or Keresan peoples occupy the pueblos of San Felipe, Santo Domingo, Cochiti, Santa Ana, and Zia, in the middle Rio Grande Valley, and Laguna and Acoma to the west. The Keres language is unrelated to other pueblo languages. See map 1.

[12] Santa Clara Pueblo has two curing societies. Individual society members are often called to treat a patient. Sometimes all the members of one society are engaged to treat a patient or to perform a ceremony for the well-being of a family or of extended bilateral relatives. At certain specified times the two societies cooperate in an elaborate ceremony to rid the village of "witches." (Hill MS.)

and secular officers, or approval of the choice of all or part of such officers by the cacique whom they have put into power. Membership in these societies is by curing, trespass, or choice, and is independent of membership in other organizations.

The characterization given above is that of contemporary Keres culture. Hawley (1950*b*, p. 511) suggests that before the Keres were influenced to any great extent by Tanoans and whites—at the time the Keres first came in contact with Tanoans—their culture may have been more like that of Zuni and Hopi. What "western traits" we perceive in the Tanoan pueblo cultures of today must be attributed mainly to the Keres. Thus it is probable that clans and the katcina cult—weakly represented among the Tanoans—were borrowed from the Keres.

When Coronado entered the pueblo country in 1540 the Tano had been in the Galisteo basin for approximately 250 years and had been exposed to at least 200 years of Keres influence. Considering the conservative nature of the pueblos, however, it is probably safe to hypothesize that the main outlines of Tanoan Anasazi culture, as described previously, still characterized the Tano pueblos of the Galisteo basin. They may have adopted the katcina cult in attenuated form, and perhaps the clan. The clan was probably functionless, as it is among the Tewa today; at any rate, some concept of the clan was probably acquired. In general, however, the major outlines of Tanoan Anasazi culture undoubtedly persisted.

We may now consider another major acculturating agency—the Spanish.[13]

Initial Contacts with Spaniards

The first contact of the Tano with the Spaniards was the expedition of Francisco Vásquez de Coronado in 1540. This was a spectacular party of several hundred mailed and armed horsemen accompanied by Indian servants.

Coronado, or members of his party, crossed and recrossed the Galisteo basin several times in the two years that they remained in the pueblo country. The impression left by Coronado and his men was not a pleasant one. The news of the execution of several hundred Indians in his headquarters at Tiguex[14] must have spread throughout the pueblo country and made the Spaniards feared and distrusted.[15] Coronado left two Franciscan friars in the pueblo area, presumably in Tiwa pueblos, when he departed for Mexico. The fate of these missionaries is unknown, but it is generally believed that they were put to death soon after Coronado's departure.

The next expedition, forty years later, was less pretentious. The party consisted of a Franciscan priest, Friar Augustin Rodríguez, two brothers of his order, and twelve volunteer soldiers under the command of Francisco Sánchez Chamuscado. Chamuscado's expedition appears to have found Coronado's Tiguex, and from near that place the party crossed the Rio Grande and followed one of its tributaries eastward to the buffalo plains. That the party came in contact with Tano pueblos

[13] The section that follows has been compiled from translated Spanish sources pertaining to expeditions that entered the Tano territory in the period under discussion. Sources consulted include Hodge, 1907; Winship, 1896; Twitchell, 1912; Hammond and Rey, 1927; Hammond and Rey, 1929; Bolton, 1916; Prince, 1912. Good brief surveys are contained in Hodge, 1912 (Pt. 2), pp. 686–687, and in Nelson, 1914, pp. 12–33.

[14] Near the present site of Bernalillo.

[15] For a minor rebellion (brought on by the incessant demands for provisions made by Coronado's party) the pueblo of Tiguex was "punished" by the execution of several hundred of its inhabitants (Winship, 1896, p. 497).

is hardly to be questioned. The friars were left among the pueblos—apparently in Tiwa pueblos—when the party returned to Mexico.

Concern for the fate of these friars motivated another expedition into pueblo country. Under Antonio de Espejo, a man of wealth, an expedition consisting of fourteen soldiers and one Franciscan priest set out for the north. When Espejo reached the Tiwa pueblo region, he learned that the friars had been killed. Although the purpose of the expedition was fulfilled, Espejo and his party remained and re-explored practically all parts of Arizona and New Mexico that had been known to Coronado. Espejo visited Zia, Jemez, Acoma, Zuni, and Hopi, and returned to the Rio Grande. He then passed east through the Galisteo basin and Tano villages to the Pecos River and returned down the Pecos to Mexico.

Espejo has left us probably the best detailed description of early pueblo villages and life. Although he tended to exaggerate the size of the populations of the Indian peoples he encountered, he was a close practical observer and an otherwise sincere reporter. His exaggerated numbers were probably given to enhance his discoveries and to impress the Crown.

A rather long quotation from Espejo's narrative is given below to show the conservative nature of pueblo culture. It is remarkable that, with only a few minor additions, the account could serve as a description of pueblo life at the beginning of this century, more than three hundred years later. Although the pueblos Espejo is describing are those of the Piro, a dialect branch of the Tiwa, he reports later (when he is among the Tano) that "they [the Tano] govern themselves as do the preceding provinces, and like the rest have idols which they worship" (Bolton, 1916, p. 180). Since both the Piro and the Tano are Tanoan pueblos, differences in culture were probably not very pronounced.

Espejo reports (Bolton, 1916, pp. 177–179):

As we were going through this province [the Piro country], from each pueblo the people came out to receive us, taking us to their pueblos and giving us a great quantity of turkeys, maize, beans, tortillas, and other kinds of bread . . . They grind on very large stones. Five or six women together grind raw corn . . . and from this flour they make many different kinds of bread. They have houses of two, three, and four stories, with many rooms in each house. . . . in each plaza of the towns they have two *estufas* [kivas],[16] which are houses built underground, very well sheltered and closed, with seats of stone against the walls to sit on. Likewise, they have at the door of each *estufa* a ladder on which to descend, and a great quantity of community wood, so that strangers may gather there.

In this province some of the natives wear cotton, cow hides, and dressed deerskin. . . . The women wear cotton skirts, many of them being embroidered with colored thread, and on top a *manta* like those worn by the Mexican Indians, tied around the waist with a cloth like an embroidered towel with a tassel. . . . and all, men as well as women, dress their feet in shoes and boots, the soles being of cowhide and the uppers of dressed deerskin. The women wear their hair carefully combed and nicely kept in place by the moulds that they wear on their heads, one on each side, on which the hair is arranged very neatly, though they wear no headdress. In each pueblo they have their caciques . . . These caciques have under them . . . *tequitatos*,[17] who are like *alguaciles*, and who execute in the pueblo the cacique's orders . . . And when the Spaniards ask the caciques of the pueblos for anything, they call the *tequitatos*, who cry it through the pueblo in a loud voice . . .

. . . In each one of these pueblos they have a house to which they carry food for the devil, and

---

[16] This may indicate a moiety system. Hawley (1950) reports, however, that the historic pueblos which have a moiety organization do not all have two kivas.

[17] This official is possibly the "Outside Chief," who is an intermediary for the cacique—one for each moiety chief among the Rio Grande Tewa—in all secular affairs and meetings with nonvillagers. The position exists in virtually all the Rio Grande pueblos.

they have small stone idols which they worship.[18] Just as the Spaniards have crosses along the roads, they have between the pueblos, in the middle of the road, small caves or grottoes, like shrines, built of stones, where they place painted sticks and feathers, saying that the devil goes there to rest and speak with them.[19]

They have fields of maize, beans, gourds, and *piciete* [tobacco] in large quantities . . . Some of the fields are under irrigation,[20] possessing very good diverting ditches, while others are dependent upon the weather. Each one has in his field a canopy with four stakes . . . where he takes his siesta, for ordinarily they are in their fields from morning until night . . . Their arms consist of bows and arrows, *macanas* and *chimales*; the arrows have fire-hardened shafts, the heads being of pointed flint, with which they easily pass through a coat of mail. The *chimales* are made of cowhide, like leather shields; and the *macanas* consist of rods half a vara long, with very thick heads. With them they defend themselves within their houses. It was not learned that they were at war with any other province. . . .

After Espejo's return to Mexico he sought royal permission to colonize. Other men also applied for contracts; and in 1590, while these proposals were being considered, there set out an unauthorized expedition under the command of Castaño de Sosa. Castaño had a group of about two hundred followers. The party went up the Pecos River to Pecos Pueblo, where temporary headquarters were established. Castaño with a small party then explored the possibilities of establishing a colony in the upper Rio Grande Valley. He went as far north as Taos, came down the Rio Grande to the Keres pueblos, and then returned to Pecos by way of the Galisteo basin. Here he named the pueblos of San Marcos, San Lucas (later called Galisteo), and San Cristóbal—names which were retained by Oñate in the succeeding period of Spanish rule.

Castaño's efforts to establish a colony were thwarted; a military force arrested him and returned him with his entire following to Mexico. The return of Castaño and his party closed the period of exploring expeditions from Mexico.

From 1540 to 1590 the Tano pueblos had been visited by five different expeditions. Although none of these groups had remained long enough to effect a pronounced change in their way of life, the Tano were undoubtedly awed and impressed by the material equipment and military strength of the newcomers. The executions at Tiguex and other atrocities committed by the Spaniards could not have endeared them to the Tano. The Tano must also have been perplexed and confused by the zealous padres who tried to convert them to a religion which had so little similarity to their own. The Spaniards were probably more feared and distrusted than desired as permanent neighbors and coresidents.

UNDER SPANISH RULE

The contract for the colonization of the northern country was finally awarded to Don Juan de Oñate in 1595.[21] The subsequent recruiting of colonists and the elaborate preparations for the trip consumed so much time that the party did not leave southern Chihuahua until January, 1598. The colonizing party consisted of several

---

[18] Espejo and his party may have seen the altar of a religious society or moiety society when it was displayed in a house during a prayer meeting. Among the Rio Grande Tewa such retreats are held every month in the house of the leader of the society (Hill MS).

[19] An excellent description of pueblo shrines.

[20] Documentary evidence of the use of irrigation by the pueblos before the advent of the Spaniards.

[21] This section is drawn mainly from the following sources: Hammond, 1926; Hodge, Hammond, and Rey, 1945; J. B. Bailey, 1940; G. Espinosa, 1933; Scholes, 1936; Scholes, 1942.

hundred Spaniards, Mexican Indians, and servants. There were eighty carts and wagons and more than a thousand head of cattle. Because of the wagons and the cattle, the train moved slowly; it did not reach the northern Rio Grande area until the year was almost gone.

Oñate preceded the main party with a troup of soldiers, and by the end of 1598 he had obtained submission of all major pueblos. Since the pueblos had no concept of territorial conquest, "submission" is probably an inappropriate word. The Pueblo Indians may have merely assented to the right of the Spaniards to settle on the land. The tribute and labor later demanded of them was undoubtedly an unexpected and shocking effrontery.

The entire country was at once divided into seven missionary districts. The Tano pueblos were placed either with Pecos or with the Keres on the Rio Grande. The first census figures in 1630 reported 60,000[22] native converts living in ninety villages, each of which had its own church. Five pueblos were said to be occupied by the Tano, and the population was given as 4,000.[23] The five pueblos were probably San Marcos, San Lázaro, San Cristóbal, Galisteo, and perhaps Cienega. It is not possible to determine from historical records whether Cienega was a Keres or a Tano pueblo; there is no question, however, that the other four villages were Tano pueblos.

The number of chapels in 1630—ninety in as many villages—indicates the force with which the Spaniards started their Christianizing efforts. With the increase in missionary activities, the tension between the pueblos and the Spaniards rose, and by the mid-seventeenth century the situation was serious.[24] Scholes (1942, p. 11) aptly describes this period:

Indian affairs during the decade of the 1650's were characterized by an increasing restlessness among the Pueblos and a growing hostility on the part of the Apache tribes.

By 1650 the Indians were fully aware of the meaning and implications of Spanish supremacy and the mission system. Spanish supremacy had brought a heavy burden of labor and tribute, and encroachment on the lands of the pueblos. The mission system added to the burden of labor, but the most important phase of the program of Christianization was its effect on the old folk customs.

The friars sought not only to teach a new faith, but they zealously tried also to put an end to the practice of native religious ceremonial, to destroy the influence of the traditional leaders of the Indians, and to impose rigid monogamy on a people whose code of marital and sexual relationship was fairly flexible and elastic. In order to maintain mission discipline the friars often resorted to the imposition of physical punishment for such offenses as failure to attend religious services, sexual immorality, and participation in the native ceremonial dances.

The Tano and Tewa, who lived closest to Santa Fe, undoubtedly supplied more than their share of tribute and services and probably suffered most severely from disciplinary measures.

In their zealous efforts to convert the conservative pueblos to Catholicism and to acculturate them to Spanish culture, the Spaniards defeated their own purposes by using force and drastic methods. The Indians resisted all efforts of the Spaniards

---

[22] A census taken by Father Benavides (Hodge, Hammond, and Rey, 1945). This was not an actual count and appears to be extremely exaggerated. Hodge (1912, Pt. 2, p. 325) estimates a population of 28,750 in 1680 for the pueblos, exclusive of Hopi. Hackett and Shelby (1942, p. xxi) estimate a pueblo population of 16,000 in 1680.

[23] This figure, also given by Benavides (Hodge, Hammond, and Rey, 1945), seems high. Hodge (1912, Pt. 2, p. 325) estimates the Tano population in 1680 at 1,400.

[24] Added to this was the constant bickering between Spanish civil and church authorities. See Scholes, 1936–1937.

to make them Christians and to change their way of life. Scholes (1942, pp. 15–16) again describes this situation admirably:

> But drastic disciplinary measures . . . could not force full allegiance to the new order. The efforts of the clergy to abolish the old ceremonial forms and to set up new standards of conduct merely caused greater resentment on the part of the Indians . . . The Pueblos were not unwilling to accept externals of the new faith, but they found it difficult to understand the deeper spiritual values of Christianity. Pueblo religion served definite material and social ends, viz., the propitiation of those supernatural forces which they believed controlled their daily existence. They expected the same results from the Christian faith. But they soon realized that the new ways were no more successful in obtaining a good harvest than the old, and they realized too that the efforts to abolish their traditional ceremonials and destroy the influence of the old native leaders whose functions were both social and religious raised serious problems concerning the entire fund of Pueblo civilization. Bewilderment soon turned into resentment, and resentment into a resurgence of loyalty to the traditional norms of folk-culture. The burden of labor and tribute might have been tolerated if offset by recognized advantages, but if the new was no more efficient in guaranteeing a harvest or success in the hunt, what had been gained by accepting Spanish overlordship?

This state of affairs finally led to the successful Pueblo rebellion of 1680. Although the revolt was planned by a Tewa religious leader of San Juan Pueblo and the actual hostilities started from Taos Pueblo, the Tano took a very prominent part. The news of the revolt leaked out before the day planned for its execution, and the revolt was put into effect prematurely. The Tano, being closer to the entrenched Spaniards in Santa Fe, laid siege to the city. They fought the Spaniards alone for five days, until reinforcements of Tewa and northern Tiwa arrived. The northern Tanoans fought bitterly and finally compelled the Spaniards to abandon Santa Fe. It is noteworthy that, although the fleeing colonists were at the mercy of the Indians, they were not attacked but were permitted to make their retreat, the Indians watching and pursuing from a distance.

Although the northern Tanoans were the most active in the revolt, the other pueblos coöperated by killing their resident missionaries and other Spaniards. The Apache seem not to have participated actively; but the Spaniards were led to believe that they were in the revolt pact and therefore succumbed more readily.

About one thousand colonists in the south took refuge in Isleta, a pueblo that remained friendly to the colonists. Believing that the Spaniards in Santa Fe and the northern area were all dead, this group finally retreated south to El Paso. The refugee group from Santa Fe, also numbering about one thousand—men, women and children—later joined the southern colonists in El Paso.

At the end of the revolt, 21 out of 33 missionaries and about 375 colonists out of a total of about 2,350 were dead.[25] All the missions were destroyed, together with their furnishings and records. The proportion of casualties among the Indians was about the same, the Tano suffering the most. In two skirmishes alone, 300 Tano besieging Santa Fe were killed and 47 were captured; the prisoners were later executed (Hackett and Shelby, 1942, pp. lxiv and lxv).

Soon after the retreat of the Spaniards, internal dissension arose among the pueblos. The Keres and the Pecos Indians became actively hostile toward the Tewa and Tano. The Apaches also became active. After the threat of Spanish intervention

---

[25] These figures are from Hodge, 1912 (Pt. 2), p. 319. Hackett and Shelby (1942, p. xx, n.) estimate a population of 2,800 Spaniards in the province of New Mexico in 1680; Scholes reports that the Spanish population at the time of the Pueblo revolt probably never exceeded 2,500.

was removed, they began to raid the marginal pueblo villages with renewed fervor. These circumstances led to the abandonment of the Galisteo basin. The Tano of Galisteo, San Marcos, and Cienega moved into Santa Fe; those of San Lázaro and San Cristóbal moved to the northern Tewa country in the vicinity of the present Santa Cruz and established two separate settlements.[26]

When Don Diego de Vargas reconquered the pueblo area in 1693, the Tano in Santa Fe submitted peaceably. A large number of them were given to the soldiers and colonists as slaves, and the rest settled among the Tewa villages, particularly in the pueblo of Tesuque. Finally, in 1706, these dispersed Tano were gathered together and resettled in the pueblo of Galisteo (Bloom, 1935). Comanche raids and epidemics of smallpox rapidly decimated the population, and between 1782 and 1794 the few surviving Galisteo Tano moved to the pueblo of Santo Domingo.[27]

Our main concern, however, is with the Tano of San Cristóbal and San Lázaro, who settled in the northern Tewa country. Here Vargas found them in 1692, and in the succeeding four years they gave him a good deal of trouble. Early in 1694 the inhabitants of the two villages, together with other northern Tewa, took refuge on Black Mesa near San Ildefonso. From this stronghold the confederates made raids occasionally as far as Santa Fe. They withstood the attacks of Vargas for nine months, but were finally compelled to sue for peace and agreed to return to their villages (Bandelier, 1890–1892, pp. 82–83).

The arrival of new colonists and the crowding of Santa Fe caused Vargas to found a new villa in the Tewa basin (J. B. Bailey, 1940, pp. 206–207). The lands of the new settlement took in the pueblos and territory occupied by the Tano pueblos of San Lázaro and San Cristóbal. The settlement was named Villa Nueva de Santa Cruz de Españoles, Mexicanos del Rey Nuestro Señor Carlos Segundo. The dispossessed Tano Indians of the two pueblos were resettled together farther up the valley in the vicinity of what is now Chimayo. The name San Cristóbal was applied to the community of both groups of Tano. This settlement is undoubtedly the site known to the Rio Grande Tewa as *c'èwaréh*—from whence the Tano, the ancestors of the present Hopi-Tewa, migrated to Hopi.[28]

By the beginning of 1696 the Indians in practically all the pueblos of New Mexico were again manifesting discontent. The missionaries in the pueblos felt the mounting tension and petitioned Vargas for garrisons. Vargas did not meet their demands but stated that any missionary afraid of his charges might return to Santa Fe. Some of the friars are reported to have left their missions and come to Santa Fe (J. B. Bailey, 1940, pp. 226–228).

Early in June some of the Tewa and the Indians of Taos, Picuris, Santo Domingo, and Cochiti and the resettled Tano of San Cristóbal rose in revolt. Twenty-one

---

[26] The same names, San Lázaro and San Cristóbal, were applied to these settlements by the Spaniards after the reconquest.

[27] Hodge (1907, p. 482) reports: ". . . [Galisteo] remained an inconsiderable village until between 1782 and 1794, when the inhabitants, decimated by smallpox and by the persistent hostilities of the Comanche, removed to Santo Domingo pueblo, where their descendants still live, *preserving the language of their ancestors and in part their tribal autonomy*" (italics mine). Bandelier (1890–1892, Vol. IV, Pt. 2, p. 102, n. 3) also reports: "It is said that the Tanos maintain a separate tribal government within the pueblo." This is interesting in view of the fact that the Hopi-Tewa have also persisted in maintaining their cultural identity. White (1935, pp. 27 and 28) met with little success in determining cultural differences between Tano and Santo Domingo Keres, though one informant stated that the Tano language has persisted among the descendants of the immigrants. White says that more data should be secured regarding Tano–Santo Domingo relations.

[28] See Hodge, 1912 (Pt. 2), p. 822, under *Tsawarii*.

Spaniards and six priests were killed, including Father Francisco Joseph de Arvisu, the resident priest at San Cristóbal. After this revolt the Tano of San Cristóbal fled west to Zuni and from there to the Hopi country.[29] From the testimony of three Indian prisoners, Vargas learned that the revolt was planned to be general, like that of the 1680 rebellion. The prisoners reported that the Zuni and Hopi had also been brought into the conspiracy. The cacique of Nambe, Diego Xenome, one of the prisoners, also declared that Cristóbal Yope, the governor of San Cristóbal, one of the leaders of the revolt, and his followers had reached Zuni and had been given food and shelter there (J. B. Bailey, 1940, pp. 226–228).

The abandonment of San Cristóbal and the western migration of its Tano inhabitants finishes the history of the ancestors of the present Hopi-Tewa in the Rio Grande area. We will resume their history in Hopi presently, but at the moment it is important to consider the effects of almost one hundred years of Spanish rule.

The zealous and coercive efforts of the missionaries and secular officials did not make Christians of the Tano and seem to have had a negative effect in changing their culture. Spanish efforts to convert and Hispanize the Tano, however, did introduce the resistance patterns that characterized the Tano until the end of the nineteenth century. This resistance to change, although initially an opposition to Spanish culture, eventually came to be an opposition also to Hopi culture. The futility of the use of force to effect changes is illustrated clearly by the failure of the Spaniards to acculturate the Pueblos. In their tenacious objection to acculturation, the Tano— and their descendants, the Hopi-Tewa—are an outstanding example of group solidarity and group resistance.

It is interesting that the Tano's resistance to change should also manifest itself archaeologically in architecture. Nelson, who excavated a number of the major ruins in the Galisteo basin, reports (1914, p. 112):

They [Tano] had the example and presumably the advice, as well as the occasional coercion, of Spanish colonists and missionaries in reference to the execution of many common tasks for nearly a century. Those who lived at Pueblo Galisteo enjoyed the privilege for about a hundred years more. Yet the architectural remains, so far examined, do not reveal any marked changes or improvements. The Tanos of historic times constructed the same style of building, retained the same room dimensions, the same sort of doors, fireplaces, etc., as their ancient forefathers.

Another aspect of Tano culture which was unaffected by Spanish culture is the political organization. It is certain that the Tano pueblos, like other Rio Grande pueblos, experienced the imposition of the Spanish system of civil government. Each Rio Grande pueblo since the early seventeenth century has appointed a set of officers to meet with outside agencies (Bandelier, 1890–1892, p. 200). These officers are usually a governor, a lieutenant-governor, sheriffs, *mayordomos*, and *fiscales*. The governor represented the village in all important dealings with the Spanish authorities. The lieutenant-governor serves as assistant to the governor and substitutes for him when he is absent; if the governor dies, the lieutenant-

---

[29] The Hopi-Tewa migration to Hopi is believed to have taken place in two groups. Their migration legend reports that one group fled to Hopi via Zuni after murdering their resident priest! The other group or faction went directly to Hopi. The San Cristóbal population, as we have seen, was formerly from two distinct Tano villages, San Lázaro and San Cristóbal. It is conceivable that in the migration the two groups went separately: possibly some Tewa also accompanied the Tano. Between 1680 and 1696 many Indians migrated to the Hopi country. In the early eighteenth century a number of Spanish expeditions went to the Hopi country to bring back these "apostates." See below, pp. 276–277.

governor succeeds him. The sheriffs maintain law and order within the pueblo, the *mayordomos* are ditch bosses, and the *fiscales* are assistants to the Catholic priest and caretakers of the village chapel.[30]

The civil organization has not, however, displaced the native sociopolitical organization in any of the Rio Grande pueblos of which we have accounts.[31] The native organization is intricately interwoven with the ceremonial and religious life of the pueblo. The civil organization is clearly secular. The officers of the civil organization are appointed by a member or members of the native sociopolitical organization and are considered subordinate to them. This perhaps was not realized by Spanish authorities, but it is clear from ethnographic accounts of contemporary Rio Grande pueblos.

Although it is quite apparent that the Tano pueblos at one time possessed a set of secular officers like that of the present Rio Grande pueblos, nothing exists in the present Hopi-Tewa sociopolitical organization to suggest it. Obviously the organization was discarded along with other Spanish nonmaterial cultural items which once may have been incorporated into the culture. In its social, political, and ceremonial organization, as will be seen, Hopi-Tewa culture is completely non-Spanish. Certain resemblances to a generalized Rio Grande puebloid culture are evident, but these are in areas where Spanish culture has had the least influence.

At Hopi

The Hopi pueblos, although a part of Spain's northern province, had much less contact with the Spaniards than did the Rio Grande pueblos.[32] This was obviously because of the distance of Hopi from Santa Fe, the provincial capital, the lack of mineral resources, and the general inhospitality of the environment. Like those of the Rio Grande pueblos, however, the contacts of the Hopi Indians with the Spaniards were decidedly unfavorable. The first Spaniards in 1540—a party of the Coronado expedition—are reported to have attacked the Hopi town of Kawaika-a because the inhabitants refused to let them in. Many Hopi were killed and the town was destroyed[33] (Hammond and Rey, 1929, p. 96 n. 101).

In 1583, Antonio de Espejo, seeking mines, passed the Hopi villages. Espejo spent six days in the Hopi country visiting all the villages. His spelling of Hopi town names are close enough to present-day renditions for us to recognize Awatovi, Walpi, Mishongnovi, Shongopovi, and Oraibi. Espejo received an enthusiastic welcome, and apparently he and his party comported themselves well (Hammond and Rey, 1929, pp. 94–104).

Oñate, the colonizer of New Mexico, next visited the Hopi in 1598 and received the formal submission of the Hopi chiefs (Hammond, 1926, p. 449). On a search for the South Sea, Oñate in 1604 and 1605 once more saw the Hopi villages. He visited

---

[30] This is a generalized presentation of "Spanish officers" and their duties. The officers differ in name, number, and functions in the various pueblos, but in each case are clearly recognizable as an imposed set of officers with duties of a secular nature.

[31] For accounts of this set of officers in other pueblos, see Goldfrank, 1927, pp. 37–41; Parsons 1929, pp. 102–107; Stevenson, 1889–1890, pp. 16–19; White, 1932a, pp. 52–55, 60; White, 1932b, pp. 19–21; White, 1935, pp. 42–47.

[32] For an excellent summary of Spanish-Hopi contacts, see Montgomery, Smith, and Brew, 1949. Good brief histories of Hopi are also to be found in Colton, 1930; Bartlett, 1934; Bartlett, 1936.

[33] Brew (Montgomery, Smith, and Brew, 1949, pp. 6 and 7) believes that this report is false. For the basis of this opinion, see Reed, 1942, pp. 119–120.

them on his way west and also on his return to the Rio Grande (Bancroft, 1888, pp. 154–157).

No references of Spanish visits to Hopi for the next twenty-five years have been found. Between 1629 and 1641, missions were established at Awatovi, Shongopovi, and Oraibi with visita chapels at Mishongnovi and Walpi (Scholes and Bloom, 1944–1945). For about fifty years the Hopi were under the mission system and, like the Indians of the Rio Grande pueblos, must have come to understand the meaning of the Spanish missionary program. Through bitter experience they must have learned that there could be no compromise between Christianity and the Hopi way of life. Realizing the strength of the Spaniards, they supplied the demands of labor made upon them. Their resistance was passive but persistent; they permitted themselves to be baptized but inwardly retained their native beliefs. Finally, when the Rio Grande pueblos successfully threw off the yoke of Spanish oppression in 1680, the Hopi coöperated by killing their resident missionaries (Hackett and Shelby, 1942, p. iii) and destroying the churches. In 1692, realizing the futility of opposing a superior force, they submitted to Vargas, the reconqueror of the northern province (J. M. Espinosa, 1940, p. 31). The rebellion of 1680 and the abortive revolts of 1696 brought refugees from the Rio Grande (Bloom, 1931, pp. 204–205). The Hopi, probably believing that with greater numbers they could resist the Spaniards most effectively, harbored these refugees. The Hopi may also have been harassed by the Utes at this time and so may have received the newcomers with greater enthusiasm.[34] Among these refugees were representatives of practically all the Rio Grande linguistic groups: Tiwa, Keres, Tewa, and Tano (Parsons, 1939, pp. 891 and 914). In the first half of the eighteenth century most of these groups returned to the Rio Grande or were absorbed into Hopi population. Only the Tano, or Hopi-Tewa, have continued to be a distinct group.

The first documentary evidence of the Tano at Hopi comes from Fray José Narváez Valverde's account of the destruction of Awatovi and the activities of a punitive expedition under Governor Rodríguez Cubero (Narváez, 1937, p. 386):

> At this time, his people being infuriated because the Indians of the pueblo of Aguatubi [Awatovi] had been reduced to our holy faith and the obedience of our king, he [Espeleta, the chief of Oraibi] came with more than one hundred of his people to the said pueblo, entered it, killed all the braves, and carried off the women, leaving the pueblo to this day desolate and unpeopled. Learning of this outrage, Governor Don Pedro Rodríguez Cubero made ready some soldiers to punish it, and in the following year of 1701 went to the said province of Moqui, taking with him the aforesaid religious, Fray Juan Garicochea and Fray Antonio Miranda. With his armed force he killed some Indians and captured others, but not being very well prepared to face the multitudes of the enemy, he withdrew and returned without being able to reduce them, especially as the Moquis had with them the Tanos Indians, who, after committing outrages had taken refuge among them and had risen at their command. . . .

Attempts to convert the Hopi, and expeditions to bring back the Rio Grande Pueblo Indians who had taken refuge among them, highlighted Spanish activities in the Hopi country for the next half century. In 1707 Governor Cubero Valdez sent a squad of soldiers to the province accompanied by Fray Juan de Mingues, but the expedition achieved no results (Thomas, 1932, p. 20).

---

[34] According to Hopi and Hopi-Tewa informants, the ancestors of the latter were invited to the Hopi pueblos in order to protect the Hopi from Ute invaders.

In August, 1716, Governor Félix Martínez went to Hopi with an army of·Spaniards and Rio Grande Pueblo Indians to bring back the refugees. In a signed statement (translated in Bloom, 1931, pp. 204–205) Martínez reported ". . . I explained to them [the Tanos and other apostates] the sole purpose for which I had come with the army, this is, that they should offer submission to the Divine and human Majesty and bring back all of the Indians who had rebelled, some in the year '80 [1680] and others in '96 [1696]; that they should return to their own pueblos whence they fled . . ."

The Tano refused to be moved from the "impregnable rock" (First Mesa) where they had established their pueblo. Martínez attacked, and in the battle that ensued, eight Indians were killed and many were wounded. Then Martínez proposed to the Walpi chiefs that they allow him to ascend the mesa and make the Tano prisoners. The Walpi cacique "made a proclamation that they [the Walpi] were already friends with the Spaniards and did not desire the friendship of the said Thanos; that they will be severely punished for the harm they have done in making war . . . that many of their people had been killed and wounded through the fault of the said Thanos . . ."[35] (Bloom, 1931, p. 218).

The Spaniards were assured that they could ascend the mesa without being molested. Apparently, however, Martínez decided that the venture would be too costly, for instead, he ordered his soldiers to destroy the crops in the fields. For five days the Spaniards ambushed and seized people, cattle, and flocks, "doing all damage possible to the Apostates." When all but a few "very insignificant" fields had been destroyed, the governor felt that "the enemies of our Holy Faith" had been properly punished and marched back to Santa Fe (Bloom, 1931, pp. 192 ff.).

Since the pueblo revolt, the Jesuits of Sonora had persistently petitioned the King of Spain to add the Hopi pueblos to their jurisdiction. In 1719 they won the region by royal order, but Apache activities between Sonora and the Hopi country prevented them from establishing missions among the Hopi (Thomas, 1932, p. 20). Later, in 1741, the royal order was repeated, but the Jesuits were still unable to establish contact with the Hopi. The Franciscans, in order to impress the Crown and to have the royal order revoked, sent a number of missionaries to the Hopi between 1720 and 1745. In 1741, two missionaries, Fray Carlos Delgado and Fray Ignacio Pino, succeeded in returning 441 apostate Tiwa Indians[36] to New Mexico and restored them to their old pueblos—Pajarito, Alameda, and Zandia—on the Rio Grande (Thomas, 1932, p. 160).

The activities of the Franciscans made the King reverse his royal order in 1745, and the Hopi once again came officially under the jurisdiction of the Franciscans (Thomas, 1932, p. 21).

Missionary efforts apparently diminished from 1745 to 1770; but in 1775 interest in an overland route from New Mexico to California again stimulated concern for the Hopi. This interest brought to the Hopi, in the summer of 1775, a keen observer and a sincere reporter in the person of Father Silvestre Vélez Escalante. Father Escalante was ordered by his superiors to seek a route to California through northern

---

[35] This is interesting in terms of the resistance pattern, which must have had its beginnings in this period of Hopi and Tano (Hopi-Tewa) relations. Apparently Martínez centered his activities on First Mesa; no mention is made of Second and Third mesas.

[36] These Indians are believed to be the former inhabitants of the ruined site of Payupki (see Bartlett, 1934, p. 58).

New Mexico and Arizona. He found the rugged country of northern Arizona and southern Utah impossible to penetrate, but he spent eight days among the Hopi and sent a detailed description of the Hopi pueblos and people to Governor Mendinueta in Santa Fe. He reported that there were seven villages: Hano, a second pueblo not named, and Walpi on First Mesa; Mishongnovi, Shipolovi, and Shonopovi on Second Mesa; and Oraibi on Third Mesa.

Of First Mesa, which is our chief interest, Escalante reported (as translated by Thomas, 1932, pp. 150–151):

> ... On the western point of the first and on its most narrow eminence are situated three of the pueblos. The first is that of Janos (there they say Teguas) who use a tongue different from that of the Moqui. It is an ordinary pueblo with its little plaza in the middle and will include one hundred and ten families. The second to the east [west?] about a stone's throw. It has only fifteen families because of the new settlement which the Moqui are making at Gualpi.[37] This is within gunshot of the second. It is larger than the two preceding ones and accommodates two hundred families. . . .

Escalante gives an account of the neighbors of the Hopi as well. He reports (Thomas, 1932, pp. 151–152):

> This province is bounded on the east by the Navajos, on the west and northwest by the Cosninas [Havasupai], on the north by the Utes, on the south by the Gila Apaches and on the southwest with others whom they call here Mescaleros ... The Moqui are very civilized, apply themselves to weaving and cultivating the land by means of which they raise abundant crops of maize, beans and chile. They also gather cotton although not much. They suffer from scarcity of wood and good water ...

Of the Hopi's nomadic neighbors, the Navaho were destined to become important. At this time their westward expansion was just beginning. In 1775 they were an unimportant tribe, not as yet a threat to the sedentary Pueblo Indians or to the Spanish settlements along the Rio Grande.

After Escalante's visit, a devastating drought occurred at Hopi (Douglas, 1935, p. 27). Taking advantage of the deplorable condition of the Hopi, the Spaniards made a final attempt to convert them. Governor Anza sent messengers, offering aid to the Hopi and inviting them to come and settle in the Rio Grande Valley. Although many Hopi are reported to have settled among the Navaho at this time, they did not accept the offer of the Spanish governor. In 1780 Governor Anza himself visited the Hopi villages. His report indicated a deplorable state of affairs. Starvation, disease, and migration to the Navaho country had drastically reduced the Hopi population. In 1775 Escalante reported an estimated Hopi population of 7,494; Anza's estimate in 1780 was 798 (Thomas, 1932, pp. 221–245).

The drought became less acute in 1781, and the next two decades were good years (Douglas, 1935, p. 27). After Anza's visit, Spanish reports about the Hopi virtually ceased. With the acquisition of increasing numbers of horses from the sedentary peoples, the nomadic neighbors of the Hopi, chiefly the Ute and the Navaho, became increasingly active. The Navaho, especially, provided a formidable and effective barrier between the Hopi and the Spanish colonists on the Rio Grande. Mention is made of a delegation of Hopi to Santa Fe in 1819 to ask for aid against the encroaching Navaho (Bancroft, 1888, p. 287).

---

[37] The new settlement was the middle village (Sichomovi) and not Walpi. This is clear in Morfi's account taken from Escalante's report sent to his missionary superior in Mexico (Thomas, 1932, p. 107).

". . . [The] Navajos being hard pressed, settled near the Moqui towns, and the Moquis sent five of their number to ask aid of the Spaniards. This was deemed a most fortunate occurrence, opening the way of 139 years [of concerted efforts to subdue and Christianize the Hopi]. It was resolved to take advantage of the opportunity, but of the practical result nothing is known."

In 1823 Mexico gained its independence from Spain, and the northern provinces automatically became a part of the new nation. The Mexican government was preoccupied with affairs nearer home and gave little attention to its subjects in the north. The Hopi were practically forgotten by the provincial government at Santa Fe, which had its hands full trying to quell the raids of the Comanche, Navaho, and Apache. Mexican aid undoubtedly would have been welcome at this time, for it is clear that the Hopi were mercilessly besieged by Utes and Navahos. Aged Hopi informants' reports of their grandparents' era tell of constant plundering of fields and capture of stock, women, and children.

Even before the annexation of New Mexico by the United States in 1848, the Hopi had been visited by Americans. Although only two American visits to the Hopi in the Mexican period are recorded, it is very likely that more Americans entered the Hopi country at this time. In the Mexican era, the Santa Fe trail became the great trade route between the eastern United States and the Southwest. Traders and trappers entered the country in large numbers, and it is hardly to be doubted that some of these hardy men reached the Hopi villages.

Joseph Meek, a trapper, records the passage of two companies of Rocky Mountain Fur Company trappers through the Hopi villages in the 1840's. Some of the party plundered Hopi gardens and upon being discovered fired upon the Hopi, killing 15 or 20 Indians (Victor, 1871, p. 153). In 1852 Dr. P. S. G. Tenbroeck, a surgeon of the United States Army, was told of another visit of Americans. This party, which included four women, was said to have passed through the Hopi villages about 1840.[38]

That the Hopi were aware of a change in government is indicated by a Hopi delegation to Santa Fe in October, 1850, to see James S. Calhoun, Special Agent for the Indians of the Territory of New Mexico. The objective of the visit was to ascertain the purposes and views of the United States government and to complain of Navaho depredations. Calhoun gave the Hopi delegation gifts and assured them that the government felt friendly toward them but could do nothing about the Navaho.[39]

Dr. Tenbroeck, the army surgeon mentioned above, visited the Hopi in 1852. In his report the Hopi-Tewa community is mentioned specifically for the first time since Anza reported his visit of 1780. Tenbroeck states:

The inhabitants [of Hopi] all speak the same language except those of Harno [Hano, or Tewa Village], the most northern town of the 3 [on First Mesa: Walpi, Sichomovi, Tewa Village], which has a different language and some customs peculiar to itself. It is, however, considered one of the towns of the confederation, and joins in all the feasts. It seems a very singular fact that, being within 150 yards of the middle town, Harno [Tewa Village] should have preserved for so long a period its own language and customs. The other Moquis [Hopi] say the inhabitants of this town have a great advantage over them, as they perfectly understand the common language, and none but the people of Harno [Tewa Village] understand their dialect. It is the smallest town of the 3.[40]

[38] U. S. Census, 1890 (U. S. Dept. Int., 1894), p. 171.
[39] *Ibid.*, p. 161.
[40] *Ibid.*, p. 171.

Also in the decade of the 1850's—the exact date and year is unknown—another American visitor passed through the Hopi town and made a similar observation of the Hopi-Tewa community (Cozzens, 1873, p. 466):

One very singular fact in connection with the Moquis [Hopi] is deserving of special mention, viz., the people of Haroo [Tewa Village], although living within two hundred yards of another large village . . . speak an entirely different language from those of the remaining six villages, and seem to have preserved their manners and customs intact, as well as their language, for centuries; and another singular fact is, that while the people of Haroo understand and can converse in the language spoken by the people of the other villages, they [the Hopi] neither understand nor can converse in the language spoken by the people of Haroo.

In 1858 Jacob Hamblin, the great Mormon explorer, visited the Hopi (P. Bailey, 1948, pp. 200 ff.). This was the beginning of a long and intimate relationship between the Mormons and the Hopi. In the succeeding years the Mormons made friends with the Hopi and attempted to convert them. The Mormons were sincere and considerate in their missionary efforts. Probably of all missionary groups that have proselyted among the Hopi, the Mormons have made the most favorable impression. Yet Mormon efforts, like those of other missionary groups, have resulted in very few converts.[41]

In the 1850's and 1860's, droughts, smallpox epidemics, and Navaho depredations made life miserable for the Hopi. They sought aid from Americans; but neither the government nor the Mormons could assist them, especially since the United States became involved in the Civil War. Appeals for relief from Navaho raids also came from the Spanish settlers in New Mexico, and finally, in 1863, Colonel Christopher ("Kit") Carson was dispatched to round up the Navaho (Hodge, 1907, p. 41). Carson succeeded in capturing and exiling the majority of the Navaho to Bosque Redondo in eastern central New Mexico; but isolated bands escaped apprehension and continued to harass the Hopi. To seek relief from the Navaho depredations, droughts, and the devastating smallpox epidemics, many Hopi migrated to Zuni and the Rio Grande pueblos. Not until after 1870 did the Navaho cease to trouble the Hopi. The severe drought conditions also passed, and the epidemics became less virulent. Gradually the Hopi population increased, and by 1904 it was reported to be 2,338. The Hopi number has continued to grow, and in 1950 it was estimated at 4,000.[42]

After the Civil War, contact with Americans steadily increased. About 1870 the first traders and Protestant missionaries arrived. A mission school was established in 1875 at Keams Canyon. In 1869 a special agent for the Hopi was appointed, and in 1882 the Hopi Indian Reservation of 3,863 square miles was set aside by executive order.[43] At the request of First and Second Mesa Indians, a government school was opened at Keams Canyon in 1887. Most of the villages were indifferent to the new school; Oraibi refused to send any children to it. Only First Mesa welcomed the school, and the majority of the children were from the Hopi-Tewa community.[44]

[41] See "Relations with Americans," in chap. ii.
[42] See "Population," in chap. ii.
[43] See U. S. Dept. Int., Annual Reports of the Commissioner of Indian Affairs for the years indicated; also Jones, 1950. The Navaho have encroached on this reservation and the Hopi have been restricted to a land-management district about one-fourth the size of the original reservation This area has been fenced and the remainder of the reservation has been turned over to the Navaho Since the original reservation has never been revised by any executive or legislative action, the Hopi still have a claim on the original boundaries of the reservation. (Jones, 1950, p. 23.)
[44] U. S. Census, 1890 (U. S. Dept. Int., 1894), p. 190.

In this period, sporadic mention is made of the Hopi-Tewa by American visitors. An interesting report of a traveler in 1872 (Beadle, 1878, pp. 266–267) indicates that the chief of First Mesa (Walpi) had a Hopi-Tewa interpreter:

At [Fort] Defiance I was told to ask for Chino,[45] the *Capitan* of this *mesa* [First Mesa], before I talked to any one else; so I shouted to call out some one.... I was greatly relieved when a tall old fellow, with a merry twinkle in his eye, arrived, addressed me in pretty good Spanish, and intimated that he did the talking for Chino when strangers came. His name, which he had on a card written by some white man, was Misiamtewah; he had visited the Mormon settlements and Santa Fe, and could speak Spanish, Moqui [Hopi], Tegua and a little English and Navajo, besides being fluent in the sign language. I cultivated his acquaintance at once.

Since Misiamtewah spoke Tewa, he was probably a native of Tewa Village and the official interpreter for the Hopi of First Mesa—which appears to be an office reserved for a qualified Hopi-Tewa.

Another reference to the Hopi-Tewa is made by Julian Scott, a special agent for the Hopi tribe in the late 1880's:

"They [Hopi-Tewa] show a pronounced difference in their bearing from the pure Moqui [Hopi], and as a general rule are taller and broader. They are foremost in all things that pertain to their future good, and were the first to leave the mesa and build new homes more convenient to wood and water and their fields."[46]

By 1885 the careful recording of Hopi life and ceremonies had begun. H. R. Voth, a Moravian minister at Oraibi, and Alexander M. Stephen, a former U. S. Army officer and resident of First Mesa from 1880 to 1893, began the systematic study of Hopi culture early in 1880. From 1890 to 1900 Dr. J. Walter Fewkes of the Bureau of American Ethnology, Washington, D.C., recorded data and published works on Hopi ceremonial life. Other students followed, contributing to a rapidly increasing body of ethnographic literature which is perhaps the most exhaustive extant on an American Indian tribe. Popular accounts, emphasizing the esoteric and colorful ceremonies of the Hopi Indians, have also been written; for many decades they have continued to popularize the Hopi. These and the colorful ceremonies themselves brought large numbers of American tourists to the Hopi mesas at a very early date and have continued to attract them. The Snake Dance ceremony alone draws a crowd of several thousand spectators annually.

The Atlantic and Pacific Railroad (now the Atchison, Topeka and Santa Fe) crossed Arizona south of the Hopi villages in 1882 (Bradley, 1920, pp. 220–221). The railroad, although seventy miles away, brought an influx of tourists and over a period of seventy years has provided employment for a large number of Hopi and Hopi-Tewa.

Wagon roads—from Gallup and Fort Defiance and later from Holbrook, Winslow, and Flagstaff—have been in existence for more than half a century. These roads have been greatly improved in recent years, and today hundreds of tourists motor through the Hopi mesas.

By the end of the nineteenth century, government day schools had been started at Polacca, Toreva, and Oraibi; a Mennonite mission was established at Oraibi in 1893 and a Baptist mission at Polacca the following year (Thompson and Joseph,

---

[45] Probably *Cimo* or *Si'mo*, town chief of Walpi who died in 1892 (see Stephen, 1936, p. 949). Tom Polacca was the "speaker" for the Walpi chief at this time (see below, pp. 285 and 295).
[46] U. S. Census, 1890, *loc. cit.*

1944, p. 29). In recent years the government has continued to expand its facilities and services. There are today seven day schools and one boarding high school that provide schooling for Hopi children. Hopi high school students may also attend the government boarding school in Phoenix. The main hospital for Hopi use is at Keams Canyon, but for emergency or serious cases, larger and better-equipped government hospital facilities are available at Tuba City and Fort Defiance on the Navaho reservation. In addition, the government has developed a program of soil and moisture conservation and has inaugurated improved farming and stock-raising methods. The Hopi superintendent, although subordinate to the regional director at Window Rock, has a great deal of independence in supervising the Hopi.

In 1936 a constitution was drawn up by the Hopi with the aid of the government, and self-government was attempted through the formation of a tribal council composed of representatives from each village. The innovation was totally unfamiliar to the Hopi, and the council has not worked out as envisaged. The Hopi have never functioned as a unit in the past and do not seem ready to do so at present. For reasons that subsequent chapters will make apparent, First Mesa culture has achieved a remarkable degree of social and political integration in recent years; but this is not true of the other Hopi village groups. The role of the Hopi-Tewa in this integration is important and will be discussed in a later chapter.

Contact with white Americans has modified the externals of Hopi and Hopi-Tewa culture profoundly. Most of the clothes, material possessions, and even food now are made by white Americans or are brought in by them. English as a secondary language is spoken by the majority of Hopi and Hopi-Tewa. Wage work and livestock raising have been added to horticultural activities and are now an important part of the economic structure. It will be seen, however, that important aspects of these cultures have been unaffected. The Hopi and the Hopi-Tewa in their social organization, ceremonials, and religious concepts differ from each other, and both stand quite apart from white American culture.

SUMMARY

The history of the Tano and their descendants, the Hopi-Tewa, has been reviewed in this chapter. It has been impossible to isolate the Tano, or Hopi-Tewa, specifically from the Hopi in the latter part of this review. For the last 250 years the two peoples have shared intimately a common environment and have faced the same kinds of problems. Furthermore, while the literature of the Hopi is extensive, that of the Hopi-Tewa is meager. The history of the Hopi-Tewa has been considered for the last 250 years, therefore, largely in conjunction with that of their neighbors.

The prominent theme in this brief historical sketch is the persistent struggle of the Tano, or Hopi-Tewa, to maintain cultural identity. Both on the Rio Grande and at Hopi they fought periodically for survival against devastating raids of nomadic tribes. For about one hundred years they resisted the attempts of the Spanish to Christianize and civilize them, and they finally migrated to the Hopi country to escape Spanish oppression. In addition to human obstacles, there were also the periodic droughts and smallpox epidemics which threatened to wipe out the small group. The survival of these people as a distinct cultural group is remarkable in the face of almost insurmountable odds.

In the chapters that follow, the relations with present neighbors will be discussed, and the degree to which Hopi-Tewa culture has been influenced by these neighbors will be revealed. Hopi-Tewa social, ceremonial, and economic organization will be described, with a view to characterizing Hopi-Tewa culture and also for the purpose of indicating the acculturative processes.

CHAPTER II

TEWA VILLAGE AND ITS PEOPLE

THE HOPI villages, of which Tewa Village is one, are situated at the terminal points of a number of finger-like projections sculptured by erosion from the southern part of Black Mesa, a high plateau extending north almost to the Utah border[1] (see map 1). The elevation of the villages is approximately 6,000 feet above the sea. The tops of the mesas are about 600 feet above the dry washes that extend southward toward the Little Colorado River. Although the main villages are still on top of the mesas, clusters of individual houses have sprung up below, hugging their slopes. From east to west the mesas on which the Hopi villages are situated have been designated in the literature and by the people in the area as First, Second, and Third Mesa. On First Mesa are the villages of Tewa, Sichomovi, and Walpi, and below the mesa is a community called Polacca. Second Mesa comprises actually two separate fingers; on the first finger, starting from the east, are Mishongnovi and Shipolovi, and on the second finger, Shongopovi. On Third Mesa is Old Oraibi, and below this mesa a more recent community, New Oraibi. Farther on, but still on top of the plateau of Third Mesa, is Hotevilla, and about one mile northeast of that village is Bakabi. A recent community colonized by members of Third Mesa is Moenkopi, some forty miles west of Third Mesa. Moenkopi is near a permanent stream, and it alone of all the Hopi villages utilizes irrigation; all the other villages depend on rain and periodic floods for farming.

Tewa Village is contiguous to and immediately northeast of Sichomovi (see map 2). Walpi, the third village, occupies a citadel position at the very tip of the mesa. Sichomovi and Walpi are connected by a narrow neck of mesa, barely the width of an automobile. Although the houses of Tewa Village seem to merge with those of Sichomovi, both the Hopi and the Hopi-Tewa are keenly aware of the boundary that separates the two villages. The inhabitants of Sichomovi and Walpi speak Hopi, and the Hopi-Tewa refer to both groups as Hopi. Yet members of at least one Hopi clan, Mustard, relate in their traditional legends that they, too, originally came from the Rio Grande. The Hopi-Tewa refer to Sichomovi as *Conimú·nèh* (Zuni Plaza). Tradition states that the first inhabitants of Sichomovi were also Tano, and that they left their homeland before the ancestral migrants of Tewa Village. Although members of the Mustard clan assert that their ancestors spoke Tano, today they have no knowledge of the language.

Walpi, in its traditions, reports long residence on First Mesa and considers itself preëminent over both Tewa Village and Sichomovi because its settlers arrived earlier. Sichomovi adheres strictly to Walpi's ceremonial calendar and is essentially a "suburb" of that village. Tewa Village alone enjoys a certain amount of ceremonial independence. But in spite of some ceremonial privileges, the Hopi-Tewa are not completely free of Walpi's ceremonial dictates. Tewa Village has quarreled with Walpi through the years and has gained certain concessions but has yielded in others. The study of Hopi-Tewa social organization reveals the nature of the adjustments the group has had to make.

---

[1] The geographical position of the Hopi reservation and the physical environment of the area have been described in several recent publications. See especially Hack, 1942, and Thompson, 1950.

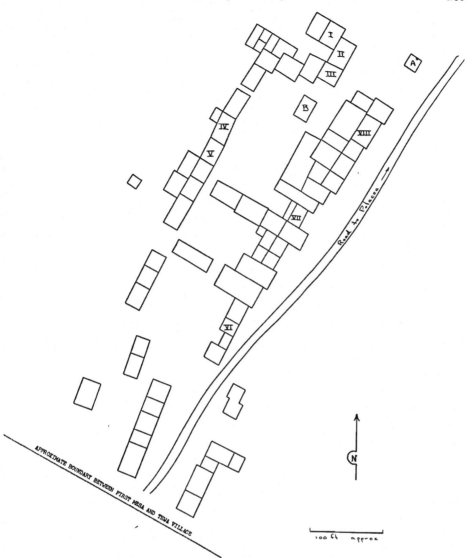

Map 2. House map of Tewa Village. Adapted from an aerial photograph by Milton Snow.

A.	Outside kiva	IV.	Fir clan house
B.	Plaza kiva	V.	Earth Clan house
I.	Bear Clan house	VI.	Cloud Clan house
II.	Corn Clan house	VII.	Sun Clan house (clan extinct)
III.	Tobacco Clan house	VIII.	Cottonwood Clan house

Below First Mesa and running roughly parallel to the villages on top is a modern community known as Polacca (see map 3), the inhabitants of which come from all three villages. Polacca was named after a Hopi-Tewa man who was one of the first to settle below the mesa. An interpreter and friend of the whites, he was persuaded by Christian missionaries to build his home away from his native village. Most of today's inhabitants at Polacca, however, are not Christians—many of them are traditionalists and own houses on top of the mesa as well. Consequently, the population of Polacca is in a constant state of flux, the inhabitants living intermittently at Polacca or on the mesa.

POPULATION

The Hopi-Tewa population[2] has more than doubled since the time of Stephen and Fewkes.[3] Stephen's census in 1893 listed only 163 persons (Fewkes, 1894, p. 165),

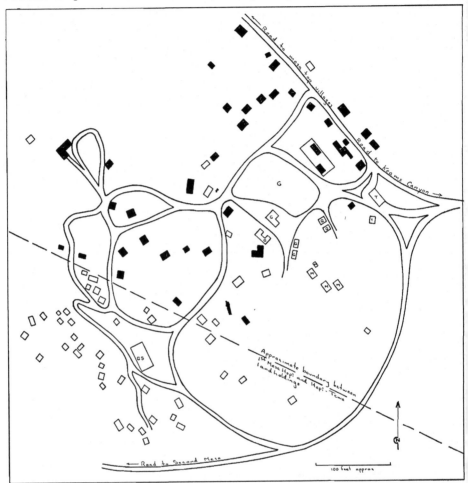

Map 3. House map of Polacca. Adapted from an aerial photograph by Milton Snow.

☐ Houses owned by Hopi women	⬛Ⓢ Government day school
⬛ Houses owned by Hopi-Tewa women	Ⓜ Mission buildings
Ⓖ Government buildings	Ⓣ Trading post

whereas my census of Hopi-Tewa individuals who belong to the Tewa Village clans is 405 (44 Hopi men and 5 other non-Hopi-Tewa men married to Hopi-Tewa women are not included in this total). The figure 405 includes those who live below the mesa at Polacca, on farms, in other Hopi villages, or off the reservation either

---

[2] The first Hopi-Tewa population was reported by Escalante in 1775 as 110 families (Thomas, 1932, p. 107).

[3] Early investigators among the Hopi. See especially Fewkes, 1894, pp. 162–167, and Stephen, 1936.

Fig. 1. Distribution of Hopi-Tewa population by clan and residence, March, 1951.

CLAN	Sex	First Mesa	Polacca	(Keams)	(residence)	(residence)	(Phoenix)	(residence)	(residence)	(residence)	(Holbrook)	(residence)	(Winslow)	(residence)	(residence)	(residence)	(residence)	(residence)	(residence)	(residence)	(residence)	(residence)	(residence)	(residence)	(residence)	TOTAL	PERSONS TOTAL
BEAR	M	5	6				2				1									1						15	31
	F	10	6																							16	
CORN	M	11	13	3												1				5	1					34	73
	F	9	15	7																8						39	
TOBACCO	M	7	8			1	4					1			1				1	2	1		2			27	51
	F	3	10				3												3	2			3			24	
FIR	M	16	8	5	2		2	1		1			4					3		2	1	5	1			50	96
	F	16	9	10		2	3					1	2									2				46	
EARTH	M	11	10		3	1	1						1	1											1	30	50
	F	10	10																							20	
CLOUD	M	1	1												1											3	4
	F	1																								1	
COTTONWOOD	M	22	9	3	4		2		1				3							3						47	100
	F	27	15				2						2							4				3		53	
TOTAL MALES		73	55	11	9	4	11	1	1	1	1		8	1	1	1	1	3	1	13	3	5	3	1	1	204	
TOTAL FEMALES		76	65	17			8					1	4						3	14		2	3	3		199	
TOTAL		149	120	28	9	4	19	1	1	1	1	1	12	1	1	1	1	3	4	27	3	7	6	4	1	405	405

TABLE 1

POPULATION DISTRIBUTION OF ALL HOPI-TEWA AND OUTSIDERS MARRIED TO HOPI-TEWA

(From my census data, March, 1951)

Residence	Hopi-Tewa			Outsiders married to Hopi-Tewa									Total out-siders	Total Hopi-Tewa and outsiders married to Hopi-Tewa
				Hopi			Other tribes			Whites				
	M	F	Total	M	F	Total	M	F	Total	M	F	Total		
Tewa Village	73	76	149	14	·	14	1	·	1	·	·	·	15	164
Polacca	55	65	120	17	4	21	·	6	6	·	·	·	27	147
Keams Canyon	14	17	31	3	2	5	·	·	·	·	·	·	5	36
Farms	11	17	28	3	2	5	·	1	1	·	·	·	6	34
Other Hopi villages	17	3	20	1[a]	15	16	·	·	·	·	·	·	16	36
Off Hopi Reservation in:														
Other Indian reservations	2	3	5	·	·	·	1	2	3	·	·	·	3	8
Parker	11	8	19 ⎫	2	6	8	1	2	3	·	·	·	11	30 ⎫
Cities	20	10	30 ⎬ 57	4	3	7	2	4	6	1	1	2	15	45 ⎬ 86
Army	3	·	3 ⎭	·	·	·	·	·	·	·	·	·	·	3 ⎭
Total…	206	199	405	44	32	76	4	16	20	1	1	2	98	503

a Wife is in violation of matrilocal residence.

on a temporary or a permanent basis; it also includes the Hopi-Tewa who have married into other Hopi villages and other tribes. Of the 405 persons, 98—49 men and 49 women—have married outsiders (Hopi, other Indian tribes, and whites). Population data are contained in fig. 1 and in tables 1 and 2. Fig. 1 shows the distribution of the Hopi-Tewa population by clans and actual residence. Table 1 gives a breakdown of Hopi-Tewa and outsiders married to Hopi-Tewa and also shows where they live; table 2 shows the number of Hopi-Tewa men and women married to Hopi, to members of other tribes, and to whites; and table 3 indicates the marital status of all Hopi-Tewa.

TABLE 2

HOPI-TEWA MARRIED TO OUTSIDERS

(From my census data, March, 1951)

	Married to Hopi	Married to members of other tribes	Married to whites	Total
Men.	32	16	1	49
Women	44	4	1	49
Total...	76	20	2	98

TABLE 3

MARITAL STATUS OF ALL HOPI-TEWA

(From my census data, March, 1951)

	Male Hopi-Tewa	Female Hopi-Tewa	Total
Married.	72[a]	72[b]	144
Divorced and not remarried.	3	8	11
Widowed	9	16	25
Unmarried and above age 30.	3	..	3
Unmarried and between 19 and 30	20	14	34
Unmarried and under age 18	99	89	188
Total male and female population..	206	199	405

[a] Of these, 9 men were divorced once and 1 man twice.
[b] Of these, 12 women were divorced once and 1 woman twice.

The Hopi-Tewa today comprise more than one-third of the population of First Mesa (about 1,000) and approximately one-tenth of the total Hopi population (about 4,000).[4]

Since Stephen's census, the process of biological assimilation has progressed along lines predicted by Fewkes (1894, p. 165), who reported that in a few years there would be no unassimilated Hopi-Tewa left. All the Hopi-Tewa today are mixed with the Hopi. Older Hopi and Hopi-Tewa recall that intermarriage was once prohibited, but there is no such restriction today.

The rule of matrilocal residence is, according to the Hopi-Tewa, strictly observed. This is true for Tewa Village but does not hold for men with their families who are living in "temporary" residences off the reservation while engaged in wage work,

[4] The 1950 Hopi Indian Agency census figures for the Hopi are as follows: First Mesa, 866; Shipolovi, 116; Mishongnovi, 227; Shongopovi, 321; Oraibi, 292; Old Oraibi, 130; Hotevilla, 427; Bakabi, 147; Keams Canyon, 102; Upper Moenkopi, 192; Lower Moenkopi, 208. These include only Hopi in residence at Hopi and not those off the reservation.

and those living in a few farming residences that are said to be "temporary."[5] These people have lived so long in nuclear-family units that they must be considered as having violated the matrilocal residence pattern.

HOPI-TEWA AND HOPI RELATIONS

Formerly a strict physical and social distance was maintained between the Hopi and the Hopi-Tewa. The feature of matrilineal affiliation and matrilocal residence practiced by both groups assured continuity of each separately, even though marriages have occurred. The primary motive for the separation, however, was strong desire on the part of the Hopi-Tewa to remain distinct. We have already seen how the ancestors of the Hopi-Tewa, the Tano, fought acculturation with the Spaniards in New Mexico and later at Hopi. This struggle to maintain cultural identity was transferred to the Hopi, and, though the pattern of resistance was undoubtedly of a different kind, it was equally as strong and effective.

The position of the Tano as a refugee group has of course fostered the perpetuation of cultural differences.[6] That the ancestors of the Hopi-Tewa were for a long time in an unfavorable position at Hopi is amply documented in myths, legends, and attitudes of the present-day Hopi-Tewa, as well as in their strong sense of village solidarity.[7] Thus, for example, the migration legend annually recited in the Hopi-Tewa kivas at the time of the Winter Solstice ceremony reports in part:

> Our grandmothers and grandfathers were not permitted to ascend the mesa when they arrived at Hopi, but were forced to make camp below. When some of them petitioned Walpi women for food, they were told to cup their hands to receive $q \cdot k\grave{e}\eta$ [a corn-meal gruel]. $q \cdot k\grave{e}\eta$, boiling hot, was poured into their hands. When the Tewa let the gruel slip to the ground and proceeded to nurse their burnt hands, the Hopi women laughed and berated them for being weak and soft.
>
> ... Our ancestors later showed them how "soft" they were by driving away the hordes of Utes that ravaged the Hopi settlements. But still the ungrateful Hopi refused to give our ancestors the land, food, and women that had been promised them as fighters for the group.[8]

The status of the immigrant Tano as protectors and warriors would not necessarily ensure them a favorable position as far as the Hopi are concerned. To the Hopi, religious preoccupation is particularly esteemed and warfare is considered uncouth and barbaric. All Hopi clan migration legends relate how latecomers were relegated to vulnerable and undesirable points of the mesa in order to meet the brunt of an enemy attack.

Another factor that would have placed the original migrant group in an unfavorable position was the land situation. Good arable land has never been plentiful at Hopi; a group as large as the incoming Tewa was undoubtedly a strain on this resource.[9]

It is therefore quite likely that from the very first the two groups were socially separate. For later periods we have ample evidence of this fact. For a long time a

---

[5] Even in the modern community of Polacca, matrilocal residence and ownership of the house by the wife have been violated in only ten instances in the Hopi-Tewa portion of the community. See map 3.

[6] Some of the accommodating devices used by the ancestors of the Hopi-Tewa to maintain cultural identity have been dealt with in a separate paper. See Dozier, 1951, pp. 56–65.

[7] See "At Hopi," in chap. i, for a quotation from the Martínez expedition of 1716. First Mesa Hopi were angry at the Tano for causing the Spanish army to attack.

[8] From the Hopi-Tewa migration legend, written in native text.

[9] See note 2.

vacant area existed between Tewa Village and the Hopi village of Sichomovi.[10] Although this area was on the Hopi-Tewa side, no one would build, "because they did not want to be near the Hopi." It was reported that children of one village were afraid to walk over the boundary line into the territory of the other.

Marriage between the two groups was restricted until fairly recent times. Thus Mindeleff (1891, p. 37) reports: "The Walpi for a long time frowned down all attempts on the part of the Hano to fraternize; they prohibited intermarriages and in general tabued the Hano."

Informants report that this restriction was equally as strong on the side of the Hopi-Tewa. The remark of one of my informants, married to a Hopi man, is pertinent:

> Our parents warned us not to play, or to have anything to do with the Hopi. Before the days of American schools, this was possible, but in school we began to associate with one another. This was true especially in boarding schools away from the reservation, where we were mingled with other Indians. Unacquainted with English and other Indian languages, we naturally sought out Tewa and Hopi acquaintances. When some of us decided to marry Hopi, our parents objected, but we married anyway. The older generation prophesied dire misfortunes in such unions, but when nothing happened in the first few marriages, more and more Tewa and Hopi married together.

Although public or plaza ceremonials were apparently never closed to one another's observation, certain kiva ceremonials were. Thus, Hopi-Tewa were not permitted in the important Hopi Winter Solstice ceremony at Walpi, and Hopi were likewise refused admittance to the similar Hopi-Tewa ceremony. In addition, certain ceremonial benefits were not extended to the other group. For example, at the time of tribal initiation ceremonies in October or November, when priests of participating fraternities came to bless the villages they stopped at the edge of Sichomovi and did not proceed to Tewa Village. Similarly, Tewa priests during the Winter Solstice ceremony blessed only their portion of First Mesa and did not go to Sichomovi and Walpi.[11]

The Tewa have emphasized in the past the factors that kept the two groups apart. They have gloried in their role as "protectors" to the unappreciative Hopi. They were careful that no Hopi observed the Hopi-Tewa kiva ceremonies, and they refused them admittance into Hopi-Tewa ceremonial societies.[12] In addition, they exploited other cultural mechanisms that fostered the maintenance of cultural separation. Thus, the reputation of the Hopi-Tewa as skilled curers was emphasized. Hopi-Tewa have long enjoyed a good practice on First Mesa, at other Hopi towns, and even among the Navaho. They proudly affirm their superiority to the Hopi in this craft.[13]

A role which is reported by both Hopi and Hopi-Tewa informants as properly and traditionally belonging to the Hopi-Tewa is that of interpreter and intermediary between the Hopi of First Mesa and all outsiders. The manner in which the interpreter and intermediary is selected I was unable to determine—apparently the Walpi town chief selects a prominent Hopi-Tewa individual, well known for his

---

[10] Shown in sketches by Victor Mindeleff, 1891.
[11] These restrictions have since been lifted. Hopi do not, however, attend the Hopi-Tewa Winter Solstice ceremony, "for the Hopi-Tewa migration legends are not pleasant to Hopi ears." See below, pp. 292 and 345.
[12] See chap. iv for additional information on membership in ceremonial societies.
[13] For further information on Hopi-Tewa curing and curers, see "The Life Cycle," in chap. iii.

eloquence and ability to speak several languages, to serve as his "speaker." At any rate, the Hopi-Tewa are proud that they alone have the ability to fill this position.[14]

The most important cultural mechanism which the Hopi-Tewa have used to maintain distinction, however, is a curse reported to have been placed on the Hopi. A legend that is often told when feeling against the Hopi runs high reports in part:

> When our ancestors had defeated the Utes and made life safe for the Hopi, they petitioned for the land, women, and food which had been promised to them. But the Hopi refused to give them these things. Then it was that our poor ancestors had to live like beasts, foraging on the wild plants and barely subsisting on the meager supply of food. Our ancestors lived miserably, beset by disease and starvation. The Hopi, well-fed and healthy, laughed and made fun of our ancestors. Finally our clan chiefs dug a pit between Tewa Village and the Hopi towns and told the Hopi clan chiefs to spit into it. When they had all spat, our clan chiefs spat above the spittle of the Hopi. The pit was refilled, and then our clan chiefs declared:

> "Because you have behaved in a manner unbecoming to human beings, we have sealed knowledge of our language and our way of life from you. You and your descendants will never learn our language and our ceremonies, but we will learn yours. We will ridicule you in both your language and our own."[15]

This curse has been extremely important in maintaining Hopi-Tewa self-esteem. It is a constantly recurring theme in traditional myths as well as in topics of conversation among the Hopi-Tewa themselves and with visiting non-Hopi Indians. The Hopi are of course aware of the curse and, moreover, firmly believe it. By the repeated assertion that the Hopi were unable to learn the Tewa language, a psychological "set" was created among the Hopi that prevented them from acquiring the knowledge. It is very curious that Hopi men who marry into Tewa Village and live there most of their lives never speak the language.[16]

Both Hopi and Hopi-Tewa feel that no Hopi should take a prominent part in a Hopi-Tewa ceremonial society. Only one society at present contains Hopi members, and it has been reported that the society will die out as soon as the Hopi-Tewa Cloud clan, which controls the society, becomes extinct.[17] There is always a feeling that Hopi membership in a strictly Hopi-Tewa society will bring about some dire misfortune. The reverse—Hopi-Tewa joining Hopi societies—is apparently not viewed with such foreboding, since many Hopi-Tewa in recent years have tried to get their children to join Hopi ceremonial societies.[18]

In spite of the trend in recent years to adapt Hopi-Tewa institutions to fit Hopi patterns, and the desire of both groups to smooth over differences, deep-rooted antagonisms persist. At the Winter Solstice ceremony, the Hopi-Tewa chiefs in each kiva tell the groups that "the Tewa were begged to come to First Mesa by the Walpi chiefs, and that they must remember this story whenever the Walpi say anything unkind to them."[19] The Hopi are not permitted to attend this ceremony since the tales told are definitely for Hopi-Tewa ears alone. At this ceremony the Hopi-Tewa

---

[14] This role of the Hopi-Tewa is discussed in greater detail at the end of this section.

[15] The legend was told to me in Tewa. The English translation is as accurate as I could make it.

[16] Hopi men married to Tewa women over a period of several years understand Tewa perfectly, however. The husband of one of my Hopi-Tewa informants is a Hopi. We habitually talk together, I speaking Tewa and he English! Under certain circumstances the language "block" is apparently removed. Another Hopi man married into Tewa Village once spoke flawless Tewa to his wife while he was under the influence of liquor. The Tewa present expressed surprise that he could speak Tewa so well and were quite puzzled about the whole affair.

[17] See "Ceremonies and Ceremonial Societies," in chap. iv.

[18] See below, p. 293.

[19] Also related by Parsons' journalist (Parsons, 1925, p. 22).

reiterate that they have their own way and that it must not be polluted by borrowings from the Hopi.

Gossip against the Hopi takes on discernibly patterned forms. The Hopi are seen as stubborn, stupid, and intellectually inferior; or they are selfish, grasping, and unmindful of the rights of others. A Hopi-Tewa interpreter related to me in Tewa his difficulty in making the Hopi understand the government order for livestock reduction:

> I explained the situation to them many times. I even drew diagrams and figures to make it easier for them to see why our herds must be reduced. The agent showed them photographs of badly eroded areas caused by overgrazing and that if this persisted all the grass would soon be washed away. He showed them pictures of superior stock with which they could replenish their own poor herds and thus with fewer sheep and cattle they could realize greater returns. I carefully interpreted the agent's words, and then repeated them over and over again. But the Hopi sat stubbornly, they could not understand. The Hopi have heads like burros!

In the winter of 1951, a Hopi-Tewa married to a Hopi man complained bitterly about some Hopi children who had come to see a dance at Tewa Village. The children had grouped about the only window, from which the family was watching the performance. The Hopi-Tewa woman exclaimed:

"Oh these Hopi, why must they always come and get in front of our window. We don't do that when we go to their villages to see dances. I think it would be better if we still lived as in our grandmother's day when we could not go to watch Hopi dances and they could not come to see ours. The Hopi have no respect for the rights of others."

Her children joined her in bitterly denouncing the young Hopi spectators outside and Hopi selfishness in general. Suddenly the mother turned, and seeing her husband sitting quietly in the room, laughed and exclaimed, "We have a Hopi right here!" Everyone laughed, and the children ran to embrace their father, who also laughed. No doubt he was familiar with this kind of talk. The conversation had been in Tewa, but Hopi men married into Hopi-Tewa households understand the language even though they never speak it.

Hopi-Tewa attitudes with respect to Hopi ritual activities appear conflicting. They vacillate between a desire to adjust to Hopi patterns and a desire to retain their own cultural institutions. The mother of a Hopi-Tewa family told me that she wanted her son to become a member of the Hopi Powamu society, but that he had refused. She said:

"I think that it is good to join in with the Hopi. We live with them and we do many things together and the Hopi religion is good. Almost everyone who joins a Hopi society recovers from an illness and lives a long time."

Several other families have expressed a desire for their children to join Hopi societies. Yet when an older Hopi-Tewa man, a member of the Hopi Powamu society, began to take an active part, Hopi-Tewa gossip denounced him. There were many phrasings of disapproval: "We have our own ceremonies; they should not be mixed with the Hopi." "If he wants to be a Hopi he should not be permitted in our kivas." "Don't let him take part in the Winter Solstice ceremony next December." Undoubtedly these warnings have limited Hopi-Tewa membership in Hopi societies.[20]

---

[20] See chap. iv, n. 30.

Hopi-Tewa when they come in contact with Rio Grande Tewa air out the feelings they bear against their neighbors. During visits of these kinfolk from New Mexico, the Hopi-Tewa go out of their way to be hospitable. Rio Grande Tewa are feted in every home, and the bonds of kin are renewed and are profusely expressed by the use of equivalent clan relationship terms. In such visits the Hopi-Tewa emphatically affirm their separatist position on First Mesa. They berate and malign the Hopi, to the amusement of their visitors.

There is considerable evidence, however, that the attitudes of hostility and antagonism are being ameliorated. For example, resistance to the Hopi way of life is stronger with the older Hopi-Tewa. At the Winter Solstice ceremony it is old men who emphasize that Hopi-Tewa must not forget Hopi injustices. Young people have much in common with the Hopi, and they tend to minimize and even laugh off these serious admonitions. Consequently, old legends tend to disappear with the passing of the aged, and young Hopi-Tewa seem content to forget them. Today, marriages between the two groups occur frequently, and Sichomovi is contiguous to Tewa Village.

Reduced friction between the two groups in recent years seems to be directly related to white contact. The unfavorable position of the Hopi-Tewa on First Mesa induced them to coöperate more readily with whites. As a result of this coöperation with whites the Hopi-Tewa became acquainted with the techniques of livestock raising and wage work. Their successes with the new economic activities brought about reduced tensions and emulation from their Hopi neighbors on First Mesa, which in turn paved the way to greater interdependence and coöperation, particularly in social and secular activities.

The important result of this contact with Americans, however, is that it has brought about a change in value orientation. Hopi culture has traditionally emphasized the sacred over the secular.[21] All activities are subordinated to religion. Horticulture, the economic base of Hopi culture, receives the full concentration of religious devotion and ritual. In an environment that is fraught with uncertainty regarding the success or failure of the subsistence economy, the religious orientation highlights "weather control."[22] Lean and bountiful years are explained in terms of faulty or successful observance of religious retreats and rituals. Activities marginal or unrelated to the basic subsistence economy receive little attention. Warfare and hunting, for example, are comparatively unimportant. Indeed, warfare may have been virtually absent before the neighboring nomadic tribes became mobile through the acquisition of the horse. When it became necessary to defend the villages against attack, the duty was assigned to late arrivals.

We can believe that events must have been somewhat as follows. The Tano, ancestors of the Hopi-Tewa, came into a profoundly religiously oriented society. The Tano religious repertoire was less complex than that of the Hopi. Its emphasis lay in curing rather than in "weather control." Tano religion was more secular because of the politically oriented moiety societies and a hundred years of Spanish influence.[23] As newcomers, the Tano were assigned the role of "protectors" in the traditionally Hopi manner. To a religion concerned primarily with "weather control" the Tano had little to contribute. Their curing societies may have been welcome,

[21] See Gillin, 1948, pp. 509–514, for an interesting discussion of this aspect of Hopi culture.
[22] See above, p. 267.
[23] See above, pp. 274–275.

but they probably had no important ceremonies to appease the harsh environment. Skill as warriors was helpful, but war was despicable and was not a prestige-bearing activity. If the Tano possessed the outgoing, aggressive personalities which characterized their present descendants, they were probably even less desired, for Hopi behavior is ideally passive.

Tano values at Hopi then must have taken literally a "back seat." The Hopi no doubt had little respect for this religiously poverty-stricken society. They did "use" the ancestors of the Hopi-Tewa, however, in the roles that they disdained—the prestigeless positions of warriors—and later used them as interpreters and go-betweens.

With the coming of the whites, the value system was altered in favor of the Hopi-Tewa. American culture is "practical" much in the same manner as Hopi-Tewa culture. In addition, the aggressive and outgoing personality of the Hopi-Tewa was more compatible with the new economic pursuits of stock raising and wage work. Religious contemplation and participation in ceremonials did not get a man a job or make him successful with herds of cattle or sheep. It is not surprising, then, that the Hopi-Tewa took to schooling, to wage work, and to stock raising with greater fervor than the Hopi. First Mesa Hopi, sensing the changing situation, began to coöperate with the Hopi-Tewa, and the reintegration of First Mesa society was begun.

The role of individuals in the changed atmosphere on First Mesa is also important. The experiences of two prominent Hopi-Tewa highlights the influence that the group exerted on their neighbors. One is Tom Polacca,[24] for whom the village at the foot of First Mesa is named; the other is Nampeyo, a Hopi-Tewa potter (Stephen, 1936, p. 130).

Tom Polacca became a prosperous livestock owner and built a large house at the foot of the mesa about the beginning of the century. It was around this nucleus that the present town of Polacca was built. Polacca learned to speak English and acted as an interpreter for the whole Hopi tribe on many occasions. He was even proposed by the government agent in 1891 to succeed the deceased town chief of Walpi. Since this position is a religious office and is hereditary within the Hopi Bear clan or its linked clans, the Hopi protested bitterly and were able to dissuade the agent from actually forcing Polacca into the position. The incident, however, is indicative of the man's prestige with government authorities.

Nampeyo's activities were perhaps even more impressive. This woman brought about a renaissance in pottery-making by copying old pottery designs excavated by Fewkes in the near-by ruins of Sikyatki. Because of its economic importance, revitalized pottery manufacture soon spread to Sichomovi and Walpi and is now the basic craft of First Mesa.

Polacca and Nampeyo shared one important characteristic: they were both traditional Hopi-Tewa,[25] participating in the ceremonies, working parties, and food

[24] For Polacca's influence on the Hopi and his ability as interpreter, see Cushing, Fewkes, and Parsons, 1922, p. 275; Stephen, 1936, p. 1117; Nequatewa, 1936, p. 131.

[25] Polacca and his family were later ostracized from the village and had to live at Sand Dunes, 5 miles from First Mesa. Polacca had sold his house and land to the Baptist mission—land to which he had only use right. See discussion on ownership and inheritance of land, property, etc., in chap. v. But during the greater part of his life Polacca was highly respected and esteemed. Until he was exiled, he was a traditionalist, following Hopi-Tewa ceremonies and filling his position as interpreter to the apparent satisfaction of all First Mesa inhabitants. In his later years he departed from the traditional pattern of life and before his death was converted to Mormonism.

Nampeyo remained in the traditional fold all her life; her status on First Mesa, once established in young-womanhood, remained high until her death.

exchanges of the community. In this respect Polacca and Nampeyo were little different from other Hopi-Tewa, and they were not considered to be deviants or outstanding persons by First Mesa inhabitants. Indeed, the fame of these two is due almost completely to their popularization by American friends. Hopi and Hopi-Tewa are rarely conscious of individual talents and achievements and do not single out individuals for special attention. Polacca and Nampeyo, in adhering to the traditional pattern of life, became submerged as individuals in the society. The fruit of their economic success was shared, however, by all the inhabitants of First Mesa through the system of exchange of food and services.[26]

The Hopi-Tewa have thus exerted tremendous influence on First Mesa, which has diffused in weaker currents to other Hopi villages. The "healthy social climate" and a generally coöperative atmosphere with the government and outsiders, noted on First Mesa by various investigators, is attributable largely to the Hopi-Tewa.[27]

Diffusion of these influences has been facilitated by the position of "go-betweens" which the Hopi-Tewa hold with respect to the Hopi on First Mesa. At present both the Hopi and Hopi-Tewa consider it the legitimate duty and responsibility of the latter to serve as interpreters and policemen and hold other positions in which they come in contact with the outside and outsiders.[28] Whether these "duties" are of recent origin or whether they were traditionally an extension of their duties as "protectors" of First Mesa is not clear. The latter reason was given to me when I asked a Walpi Hopi to explain the situation to me:

"The Hopi-Tewa are our 'speakers.' It is not right for a Hopi on First Mesa to talk with outsiders; our duties are sacred and our powers will become lost if we have any contact with outsiders. It is the responsibility of the Tewa, as it is their duty to protect us from enemies, to do our talking for us."

My own belief is that these "duties" are a recent reinterpretation by the Hopi-Tewa of their traditional responsibilities of "protecting" the Hopi. My data indicate that the political integration evident on First Mesa is quite recent, and that the assumption of "go-between" functions by the Hopi-Tewa has been a major factor in the achievement of political-secular integration.

That the Hopi of First Mesa insist on Hopi-Tewa interpreters is borne out by a recent experience of the superintendent of the Hopi Agency in a meeting on First Mesa. Since the superintendent could not locate the regular interpreter, a Hopi-Tewa Indian, he brought along a Walpi Hopi who spoke very good English, to interpret for him. But the group flatly refused to go on with the meeting unless the Hopi-Tewa interpreter could be secured. The superintendent complied, but it was very late that night before he located the usual interpreter and the meeting was resumed.

In addition to the influences exerted by the Hopi-Tewa and the working relation-

---

[26] The exchange system equalizes the standard of living to a remarkable degree and prevents the concentration of wealth in a few families. The constant interaction between the peoples of First Mesa also facilitates the dissemination of new knowledge and craft skills. See chap. v for a discussion of this important aspect of Hopi and Hopi-Tewa culture.

[27] See especially Thompson, 1950, pp. 78–80. Thompson does not, however, attribute this situation to Hopi-Tewa influence but to the fact that the First Mesa villages have "retained most of their socio-ceremonial system relatively intact." Her disregard of the role played by the Hopi-Tewa in the cultural-change processes of the people of First Mesa and the Hopi generally is unfortunate.

[28] Oliver La Farge was told at Shongopovi, at the time of the drafting of the Hopi Constitution, that the sequence in all new things was first the Hopi-Tewa, then First Mesa as a whole, then the body of the tribe (La Farge, personal communication, January, 1950).

ships developed by Hopi and Hopi-Tewa, other factors—such as boarding and day schools, government and off-reservation employment—in which Hopi mingled with Hopi-Tewa, had much to do with the lessening of friction between the two groups. Today there is constant interaction and coöperation between them. Intermarriages and the acquisition of relatives on both sides have intricately related all the people of First Mesa. The selection of ceremonial sponsors is reciprocal and helps to cement the two peoples.

It will be seen in later chapters that American contact has not profoundly changed the social organization of the Hopi-Tewa. The Hopi-Tewa and the Hopi of First Mesa have succeeded remarkably well in adjusting their traditional social culture to the changing conditions.

HOPI-TEWA AND NAVAHO RELATIONS

Considerable interaction takes place between Navaho and Hopi-Tewa. During the summer, in cattle and sheep camps, prolonged social contacts with neighboring Navaho families are maintained. There are, as well, important trade relations throughout the year. From such associations many Hopi-Tewa have acquired great facility with the Navaho language. These contacts have also provided opportunity to learn Navaho songs and ceremonies as well as to make the observations necessary for burlesquing Navahos in the winter kiva dances. A form of the *Yeibichai*—part of the Navaho Night Way—is performed every winter as one of the series of night katcina dances.

Every Hopi-Tewa home is open to frequent Navaho visitors, but the Navaho are often treated as poor relations. While the best eating and sleeping accommodations are provided for visiting Pueblo Indians, Navahos are often made to eat on the floor and to sleep outdoors.

The stereotype of the Navaho, in Hopi-Tewa conception, is a long-haired, mustachioed individual, with a kind of stupid amiability; he is absolutely irresponsible, lazy, and always extremely dirty and unkempt. A Hopi-Tewa who is careless about his appearance and clothing is often accused of being "just like a Navaho."

In spite of these attitudes there is considerable friendliness between the two groups. The services of the two Hopi-Tewa medicine men are much sought by the Navaho, and the medicine men bestow the same careful attention on the Navaho as they do on Hopi-Tewa patients. In recent years there have also been marriages between Navaho and Hopi-Tewa.[29] These Navaho spouses are respected and well liked. Curiously, these Navaho learn Tewa and speak it, for there is no tradition prohibiting Navaho from learning and speaking the Tewa language.

What disrespect the Hopi-Tewa have for the Navaho is usually mentioned only among themselves and their Hopi neighbors, always away from the hearing of the objects of their ridicule. Undoubtedly, unkind feelings toward the Navaho have been heightened by the reduction of the Hopi reservation to only about one-fourth of the area designated in the original executive order. Increase in landholdings for the Navaho was thus at the expense of the Hopi's and Hopi-Tewa's economic activities in horticulture and livestock (see Jones, 1950, pp. 17–25).

The former position of the Navaho as raiding enemies seems to be not particu-

---

[29] Two Hopi-Tewa women and five Hopi-Tewa men are married to Navaho.

larly important in Hopi-Tewa and Navaho relations today. Time has apparently removed the fear and hostility the Hopi-Tewa must have held at one time for the Navaho. Hopi and Hopi-Tewa alike speak deprecatingly of the Navaho's warfare prowess. An old Hopi-Tewa[30] whom I asked to tell me about Navaho raids said:

"The Navaho were never much trouble. They came and plundered our gardens, but they were afraid to attack us in the villages. They would sneak into our fields to rob us of our corn or go into the corrals to steal our livestock. If we surprised them in their sneaking attacks, they ran off, afraid to fight us. They only raided on horseback, for we could always outrun them on foot. A Navaho is always slow on his feet."

That the Navaho have Hopi admixture and that both Hopi and Hopi-Tewa have Navaho blood is admitted. "That is why some Hopi and Hopi-Tewa are lazy and irresponsible," a Hopi-Tewa informant told me. This same man was reputedly of Navaho ancestry!

It has already been noted that in the past considerable resentment was manifested toward the Hopi; today it is the Navaho, the tourists, and the missionaries who are most often the butt of jokes.

RELATIONS WITH AMERICANS

Hopi-Tewa, like the Hopi, have extensive social intercourse with missionaries, employees of the Indian Service, traders, and tourists. These contacts have had important influences on the Hopi, though not always in the direction envisioned by the whites.

Protestant missionaries have been in constant contact with the Hopi since just before the beginning of the century.[31] The Hopi-Tewa and the Hopi receive them passively. Converts are few, and it is doubtful whether any individual really embraces a religious denomination to the satisfaction of that sect.[32] Missionaries are received with courtesy in the homes of many Hopi-Tewa, but the attitude is one of polite tolerance.[33] Perhaps this attitude can best be illustrated by one of my experiences. Newly arrived from my home in Santa Clara, I was invited into a Hopi-Tewa home and had just sat down. The family included man, wife, and one adopted youth about twenty years old; but present also were several visitors. Just as everyone was bubbling over with enthusiasm, listening and conversing in the native tongue with a linguistic kinsman, a group of missionaries came in, apparently through previous arrangement with the household. The whites—three women and a man—brought in a kettle, fruit, and fruit jars, to give a demonstration in canning.

---

[30] This man is said to be the oldest man on First Mesa; he asserts that he was alive when the Navaho were raiding Hopi settlements. Warfare as a living branch of Navaho culture existed until about 1870, according to Hill (1936, p. 3).

[31] There are three Baptist missions on the Hopi Reservation: at Polacca, Toreva, and Keams Canyon; two Mennonite missions: at New Oraibi and Bakabi; and a Protestant mission of undetermined affiliation at Sichomovi, conducted by a native Hopi missionary.

[32] At Oraibi the missionaries have apparently exerted considerable influence. See Thompson, 1950, pp. 77 and 136–141.

[33] Parsons' journalist, a Hopi-Tewa man, suppresses missionaries by ignoring them, a very characteristic behavior of the Hopi-Tewa toward people they do not like. Parsons (1925, p. 8) reports, ". . . our Journalist has counselled the pose of indifference, of suppressing by ignoring [the missionaries]. 'Let them alone, have nothing to do with them, don't speak to them,' he advises, as determined an exponent of passive resistance as might once have been found, let us say in Germany. Even in the journal, Crow Wing [the journalist] carries out his policy. Not a word about the missionaries. They are negligible and ignored."

I arose, thinking that a pause was in order while appropriate explanations were given to the missionaries about my presence. But I was urged to sit down and resume my talk, with a perfunctory explanation that they were "only Christ people." The missionaries apparently were used to being ignored and went about their work. We kept on a lively discussion while the missionaries took over the kitchen. About an hour later the missionaries came into the room and passed around hymn books. Everyone took one politely and when a page number was announced turned to that page but continued the conversation in Tewa. The missionaries struck up a song, but still the conversation went on. Three songs were sung, with only the missionaries singing. Then one of their members started to give a talk; still we went on with our conversation. Several times I stopped, believing that out of politeness we ought to keep silent until the services were over. But each time I was told to ignore the "Christ people." Finally, in the midst of the sermon, two of the small children playing about their mothers started a fight, one of them starting to howl. To be heard above the din of crying and our own enthusiastic conversation, the missionary had to raise her voice considerably. Finally, the missionaries, having delivered two more sermons, retired to the kitchen. Realizing how late it had become, I announced that it was time for me to go. The Hopi-Tewa implored that I stay, then, realizing that I was determined to go, led me to the door. All the Hopi-Tewa said how much they had enjoyed my visit, but nothing was said about the performance of the missionaries, which had taken place in the same room.

The behavior toward missionaries was later explained to me:

It is best to be polite to missionaries, let them come in and preach. We will go on with what we are doing. It is not good to drive anyone away; we must be nice to people no matter who they are. But we feel that no one should disturb what we want to do. If they urge us to listen, we say nothing. Sometimes they talk a long time telling us that our dances are evil and that we must stop them. They say unless we go the "Christian Road" we will not be saved. But we just keep quiet and they get tired after a while and leave us alone.

One of my Hopi-Tewa friends, a woman in her fifties, when asked about participation in the weekly sewing classes conducted by the Baptist mission remarked:

We like to go to the sewing class because we learn many things there and we get a chance to talk to one another. I don't know why they are always asking us to be baptized and "receive the Lord." I do not mind getting baptized—it is only water anyway—but I don't see why I have to stop seeing the beautiful Hopi and Hopi-Tewa dances just because I get baptized. When they start asking us to be baptized we just sit quietly and lower our heads until they talk about something else. Then we stay away for a few more meetings and go again when they have stopped asking us to be baptized.

This same woman, when asked if she knew of any person that was a good Christian, replied:

I don't know about the Hopi-Tewa who live away from here, but all the people from this pueblo take part in the katcina and social dances, or they watch them. They say that if you are a good Christian you should not dance or even look at the dancers. There is one woman, R.N., who said she had become a Christian and was not going to see the dances any more. R.N. stayed away for one year, but last winter she went with me every night to the night dances. They say that R.N. is a good Christian again this year and will not come to see the dances, but I think she will be back.

The pressure on American Indians by missionaries trying to induce them to become Christians is not strong at present. In stressing the right of Indians to practice their own religion, the Indian Bureau has apparently discouraged the aggressive proselytizing efforts of the missionaries. The Hopi-Tewa do not express hostility toward the missionaries and do not seem to consider them a serious threat to their way of life.

Hopi-Tewa and Hopi do most of their buying in the trading posts.[34] Prices are extremely high; but it is a convenient way to buy, and many have charge accounts of long standing in these places. The traders are generally held in higher esteem than missionaries or many of the Indian service personnel, since traders do not try to persuade them to change their way of life.

In the summer, and less frequently in the winter, many tourists come to visit the Hopi villages. They are harmless, curious people who buy pottery and seem to like the dances. They are called *P'óhp'ò·pí?iŋ*, unbaptized ones, because they do not object to Indian dances, and seem to enjoy them. Since they are unlike the missionaries, who are critical of the ceremonies, they are held in higher regard. There is no resentment toward white visitors at either Hopi-Tewa or Hopi dances. Both groups feel that all share in bringing about good, the spectators as well as the dancers. Hence, as long as tourists are well behaved they are not resented. The remark has often been made:

"My, this dance certainly drew a lot of white people; many of them came thousands of miles just to see our dance. It is good; we do not object to them."

Many of the Hopi-Tewa work and live at Keams Canyon,[35] the Hopi Indian Agency. Here many of them have been profoundly affected by American culture. In two highly acculturated families, the language spoken in the home is English, and the children do not know Hopi or Tewa. In one of these families, the father is Hopi-Tewa and speaks Hopi and Hopi-Tewa; the mother is Hopi, but she was raised by missionaries and does not speak her native language. In the other family, the father is Hopi and the mother Hopi-Tewa; both can speak Hopi, and the mother speaks Tewa as well, but "for the sake of the children" they speak English in the home.

The Hopi-Tewa have since the late nineteenth century felt the value of coöperating with government representatives and with white people in general.[36] These relationships have had for the most part a positive effect on Hopi-Tewa culture, but certain disintegrating factors are also emerging as a result of increasing contacts with Americans and American institutions. Thus, for example, a serious incompatibility is evident between the younger, school-trained generation and the older, traditionally reared group. Off-reservation government and missionary boarding

[34] In 1944 there were 16 licensed traders on the Hopi Reservation. Three trading posts were operated by white traders, the rest by Hopi (Thompson and Joseph, 1944, p. 137). The Hopi-Tewa do most of their buying in the First Mesa and Keams Canyon trading posts. In 1951 there were two trading posts on top of First Mesa—one in Sichomovi and one in Tewa Village—both operated by native traders. At Polacca, below First Mesa, is a large trading post operated by a white trader who also operates another large post in Keams Canyon. A second trading post in Keams Canyon is also operated by a white trader. Hopi and Hopi-Tewa show no preference for either the native- or the white-operated trading posts, except that for large purchases they usually go to the white trading posts, for those are larger and have a greater variety of goods.

[35] Of the four Hopi-Tewa men married to outsiders and working at Keams Canyon, three live there with their families and one does not. The two outsiders married to Hopi-Tewa women and working at Keams Canyon live there with their families, and the two Hopi-Tewa men married to Hopi-Tewa women and working at Keams Canyon also live there with their families. Of the five widowed or divorced persons who work in Keams Canyon, four live there and one does not.

[36] U. S. Census, 1890 (U. S. Dept. Int., 1894). For quotation from this reference see above, p. 281.

schools are blamed by the Hopi-Tewa for this situation. The report of a mother of a nineteen-year-old high school girl sums up this problem:

Povi, my daughter, has been in the mission school at ——— for four years. When she finished at the day school in Polacca she wanted to go on with her studies. I told her she ought to go to the Oraibi high school where she would be near home and would come home every weekend and also for our important ceremonies. The children who go to the Oraibi school do not become mean and disrespectful to the old people and our ceremonies. After finishing at Oraibi, these boys and girls work hard and take part in the ceremonies just like the rest of us. But those who go off the reservation return bad and mean. They do not like our way of life and tell us that our dances and ceremonies are bad.

I talked with Povi about these things, but she was determined to go to the mission school where her friends were going to go. She said that they learn more at that school and that her teacher had told her it was a very good school. She prevailed on her father and her brother to let her go. My sister who has a daughter in the mission school said the school was strict and kept the girls from misbehaving. I did not want Povi to go away so far, since she is the only daughter I have, and because I have seen what happens to the boys and girls who go away to school. I talked about these things, but Povi and my sister told me that I was just trying to keep my daughter from getting good schooling, so finally I said all right, she could go.

The mission school will not let the children come home more than two times during the school year, so I was very lonely that first year. I looked forward to the summer, when Povi would be home for at least three months. I was happy thinking that my daughter and I would do many things together. But when Povi returned I found her very much changed. She had cut her hair, and it could not be put up in the "wheels" which young unmarried girls in my day used to wear and which are still worn on ceremonial occasions. Povi objected to grinding corn and making piki. She would not even take food to the kiva for the men in retreat there. She did not want to go to the ranch when we went there in the summertime, but finally went after much persuasion.

This behavior of my daughter has increased through the years. We are like strangers living together, not understanding each other. Povi is sullen and unhappy in the house. She complains of the lack of water, about our food, about our dishes and utensils. Only when we return to the mesa for the important ceremonies like the Niman and the Snake Dance during the summer is she happy, and then I hardly see her. She and her friends watch the dances and go to the trading posts, where they meet boys who, like themselves, have gone away to school. When work is to be done around the house, she is not to be found. The boys who have gone to school away from the reservation are also disrespectful and mean, and we cannot control them. They refuse to listen to the older people and do not mind their grandmothers. They talk of things that we do not understand.

We are sad that this has happened to our daughters and our sons. We have big arguments and we scold them, but this is not good, for if we have bad feelings we do not get the blessings from our ceremonies and our dances.

At present this dissident group is small. In 1951 there were only ten children from First Mesa in off-reservation schools, six of whom were Hopi-Tewa. The group does not consist entirely of persons trained in off-reservation schools, however; several returned veterans and children of families who have lived in towns outside the reservation have added to the number. Consequently there is a group of about twenty or twenty-five persons on First Mesa who habitually associate with each other. Mainly youths from seventeen to twenty-five, they loiter in the trading posts and at favorite spots along the protecting eaves of the cliffs on First Mesa. Sometimes girls like Povi are drawn into the group. This is the group that takes to drinking and often gets into trouble and then must appear before the tribal council judge at Keams Canyon. Drinking is not a serious problem at present, however; the fact that liquor must be bought in off-reservation towns and brought seventy-five miles to the Hopi mesas has undoubtedly prevented its abuse. In addition, the rich ceremonial cycle provides sufficient satisfactions to discourage the use of liquor as a substitute for recreational outlets.

The number of Hopi and the number of Hopi-Tewa in this dissident group are about equal, but in 1951 at least the ringleaders were Hopi-Tewa. Not all members of the group are die-hard iconoclasts; family and community pressures bring many of them to participate in traditional activities. Still, the attitude of the group generally is to look with disfavor on Hopi and Hopi-Tewa ceremonies and to make carping criticisms of Hopi and Hopi-Tewa life.

It is difficult to suggest a satisfactory solution to this problem. The schools, particularly off-reservation schools, have little understanding and respect for traditional Indian folkways. Students are constantly told that the Indian way of life is backward, insanitary, and in all respects inferior to American life. Not only in the schools but also in daily contacts with Americans, young Hopi and Hopi-Tewa living in off-reservation towns are made to regard their cultural heritage as a decadent way of life. At home the traditionalists feel that anyone who rejects the Hopi and Hopi-Tewa way of life is "bad" and "mean." To effect conformity to traditional living, scolding and community pressures are employed. The result is greater resentment on the part of the small but increasing group of young dissidents and a widening of the gap of misunderstanding between them and the traditionalists.

LINGUISTIC ABILITY

The Hopi-Tewa are completely bilingual in Hopi and Tewa. They change from one language to the other with great facility. In homes where both parents are Hopi-Tewa, the children constantly speak Tewa, learning to speak Hopi only through their playmates. If the father is Hopi, then the children learn Hopi simultaneously with Tewa, although they generally prefer to speak Tewa among themselves. Hopi married to Hopi-Tewa, however, never speak Tewa. The reason for this, as reported by Hopi and Hopi-Tewa informants, has been discussed previously.

Almost all Hopi-Tewa have some knowledge of Navaho speech. Some of them, particularly those who constantly come in contact with Navaho on farms and ranches, speak excellent Navaho. According to both Hopi and Navaho, the Hopi-Tewa speak better Navaho than their Hopi neighbors.

Except for a few of the very old, most of the Hopi-Tewa both speak and understand English. The younger ones, because of more schooling, of course speak English better than their elders.

MODERN EDUCATION

All Hopi-Tewa up to the ages of seventy or seventy-five have had some schooling; the younger ones have had more opportunity to acquire an education. Almost all of them complete schooling through the seventh grade, as provided in the day school. Most of those who finish day school go on to the Oraibi high school, though some go to boarding schools in Phoenix, Albuquerque, or Santa Fe. A considerable number also go to the Presbyterian Mission School at Ganado. Few complete high school; most stop usually after a year or two.

SOCIAL AND RECREATIONAL ACTIVITIES

During the winter months the ceremonial calendar is full, and coöperative activities of all kinds bring the people together.[37] With the harvest carefully stored away and

---

[37] See chap. v for descriptions of these coöperative activities.

the work of herding cattle and sheep reduced to a minimum, most of the Hopi-Tewa families come back to Tewa Village to spend the winter. Kiva dances occur weekly; in between times there are continuous rehearsals for men, while the Hopi-Tewa women are occupied with the preparation of food.

This is a time of constant social interaction. There is visiting in the evening; stories are told and experiences recounted. Most of the talk and activities, however, center around the kiva dances; the last performances are discussed while the next one is planned and eagerly anticipated.

Early in the spring the ceremonial cycle wanes. Planting and work with sheep and cattle keep entire families occupied away from the mesa. There are only two major ceremonies in the summertime—the Niman Katcina and the Snake Dance (or Flute Dance in alternate years).[38] For these events, families that have been away in cattle and sheep camps return, but for only a few days. As soon as the ceremonies are over they are back at work. These two ceremonies, however, are eagerly anticipated, and they provide considerable social interaction not only among themselves but with hundreds of visitors—whites, Navaho, and Pueblo Indians.

Acculturated families[39] and those subsisting on wage work participate in recreational activities supplied by government supervisors and Christian missions. These consist of periodic American social dances, basketball games, and weekly movies. The Baptist church conducts a weekly sewing class, which draws a small group of irregular participants. But even these people seem to find the social interaction, ceremonies, and coöperative activities on top of the mesa more satisfying. In the winter of 1951 I saw a large number of the winter katcina dances held in the kivas at Tewa Village. I was impressed by the fact that the Hopi-Tewa families working and living in Keams Canyon regularly attended these ceremonies. Since these winter dances now occur regularly on Saturday nights—a concession made specifically for wage workers—some of the Hopi-Tewa families living on job locations in Holbrook, Winslow, and Flagstaff also come to see them from time to time. The sacrifices that these people make to attend Hopi-Tewa ceremonies and renew kinship ties are indicative of the strength of traditional Hopi-Tewa culture.

Summary

Tewa Village and its people are at first glance hardly distinguishable from the other two communities on First Mesa. The architectural features of the village are of the same pattern. Houses, kitchen utensils, clothing, and other material cultural possessions differ hardly at all in the two societies. Through a long period of intermarriage the Hopi and Hopi-Tewa have also become physically homogeneous.

Important differences will appear to the keen observer, however. One obvious and clear distinction between the Hopi-Tewa and their neighbors is linguistic. The Hopi-Tewa are completely at home in both languages, Tewa and Hopi. Another

[38] Both are Hopi ceremonies; the Hopi-Tewa, although they do not actively participate in the ceremony proper, prepare food to be given to Hopi participants according to linked-clan and Hopi marriage ties. The Hopi-Tewa also act as hosts and feed visitors.

[39] That is, those families whose members have had considerable schooling or contact with American culture and who are generally sympathetic to Americans. Not all such families have abandoned the traditional way of life; many take an active part in ceremonies and participate enthusiastically in the cooperative enterprises. Most of the families of wage workers either in Keams Canyon or in off-reservation towns would fall into this category. In this group there are about fifteen families of the nuclear type; when they get back to Tewa Village they revert into the larger extended households. See fig. 1 and table 1.

important difference is in basic attitudes. This has been made clear in the section "Hopi-Tewa and Hopi Relations." The most important differences, however, are yet to be discussed. These are in areas of social and ceremonial organization, where subtle but clear differences appear.

For the moment it is important to bear in mind that a definite trend toward the integration of all three communities on First Mesa has been established. This change appears to have been brought about by contact with Americans and American values. However, American values have merely acted as a catalyst in this change. Traditional Hopi and Hopi-Tewa religious life has not been displaced; indeed it is still strong and satisfying to the people. It will also be seen in the following chapters that social organization and ceremonial ritual have been little affected by American contact. Thus a movement toward greater cohesion seems to have been launched on First Mesa without disrupting traditional patterns by substituting new ones. This aspect of the study will be discussed in greater detail in the concluding chapter.

CHAPTER III

SOCIAL ORGANIZATION

THE MOST important features of Hopi-Tewa social organization are the kinship and clan systems. Indeed, survival of the generalized Hopi and Hopi-Tewa culture depends primarily on the continuity of these institutions. In spite of their importance today, however, the current kinship and clan organizations are probably not indigenous to the Hopi-Tewa but were borrowed from the Hopi with the attendant by-products of matrilineal emphasis and matrilocal residence. The kinship system, although it differs from the Hopi terminologically and in certain behavioral aspects, is structurally like that of the Hopi.[1]

The clan too, in spite of minor differences, resembles the Hopi clan in all its essential features. Thus, the Hopi-Tewa appear to have adjusted their social organization to that of their Hopi neighbors quite early in their history on First Mesa.

KINSHIP

The following discussion of the kinship and clan systems is patterned after Eggan's masterly presentation (Eggan, 1950, pp. 139–175), in order to provide a convenient method for comparing the two descriptions. My presentation provides additional materials and indicates points of difference in both data and interpretations; in general, however, my study corroborates Eggan's conclusions.

KINSHIP TERMINOLOGY

Hopi-Tewa kinship terms, in comparison with the classificatory Hopi terminology, are highly descriptive, but the classification of kin in terms of behavior is much like that of the Hopi. The terms are in native Tewa, except for kà·káh (older sister), which was apparently borrowed from the Hopi.

Spier (1925, pp. 71–78) has classified the Hopi-Tewa system as "Crow Type," the same as Hopi and Laguna. Eggan (1937, p. 93, table 2) classifies all kinship systems of the western pueblos—Hopi, Hopi-Tewa, Zuni, Laguna, and Acoma—as the Crow subtype of the "Lineage" type.

The terminology used in the discussion that follows is shown in chart form in figs. 2 and 3. In the ascending female line a man differentiates his older sister, kà·káh, from his younger sister (sibling), tiyê·. Mother is called yíyah. Mother's older sister, káyê·, is distinguished from mother's younger sister, kó?ô·.[2] Mother's mother, sayâ·, is classified with mother's mother's sister; but a special term, pahpâ·, exists for mother's mother's mother. A man also distinguishes his older brother, píp'î, from his younger brother (sibling), tiyê·. All other senior males of the lineage[3] are classified as mother's brother, mɛmɛ́h, except mother's mother's brother and mother's mother's

---

[1] Structurally the Rio Grande Tewa kinship system is a bilateral generational one; whereas the Hopi-Tewa kinship is like the Hopi, organized on a lineage principle (Harrington, 1912, pp. 472–408; Eggan, 1950, pp. 152–153).

[2] Eggan (1950, p. 141) does not make this distinction between mother's older and younger sisters; he uses only the term kó?ô· for any sister of mother. The distinction is made by Freire-Marreco, 1914, pp. 275 and 282. Members of the household in which I lived used the terms consistently as I have them.

[3] Lineage in this discussion refers to the living descendants of a living or known common ancestress.

EXPLANATION OF SYMBOLS USED IN FIGURES 2 AND 3

These letter symbols are abbreviations of the English Hopi-Tewa phonetic terms shown immediately below them in the charts. The "L" in the final position indicates the junior reciprocal; e.g., GMBROL is "grandmother's brotherling," the junior reciprocal of "grandmother's brother."

Symbol	Translation	Symbol	Translation
FA	Father	GMBROL	Grandmother's brotherling, junior reciprocal of GMBRO
FABRO	Father's brother		
FABROL	Father's brotherling, junior reciprocal of FABRO	MANCH	Man child
FAMO	Father's mother	MO	Mother
FASIS	Father's sister	MOBRO	Mother's brother
FML	Father's motherling, junior reciprocal of FAMO	MOBROL	Mother's brotherling, junior reciprocal
FRL	Female relative-in-law	MOMOSIS	Mother's mother's sister
GF	Grandfather	MOOLSIS	Mother's older sister
GFL	Grandfatherling, junior reciprocal	MOOLSISL	Mother's older sisterling, junior reciprocal of MOLSIS
GFSISL	Grandfather's sisterling, junior reciprocal of grandfather's sister	MOYRSIS	Mother's younger sister
		MOYRSISL	Mother's younger sisterling, junior reciprocal of MOYRSIS
GFWO	Grandfather woman, or mother's father's sister, or father's father's sister	MRL	Male relative-in-law
		MYCH	My child
GGM	Great grandmother	MYMAN	My man (my husband)
GGML	Great grandmotherling, junior reciprocal of GGM	MYWO	My woman (my wife)
		OLBRO	Older brother
GM	Grandmother	OLSIS	Older sister
GML	Grandmotherling, junior reciprocal of GM	WOCH	Woman child
GMBRO	Grandmother's brother	YRSIB	Younger sibling

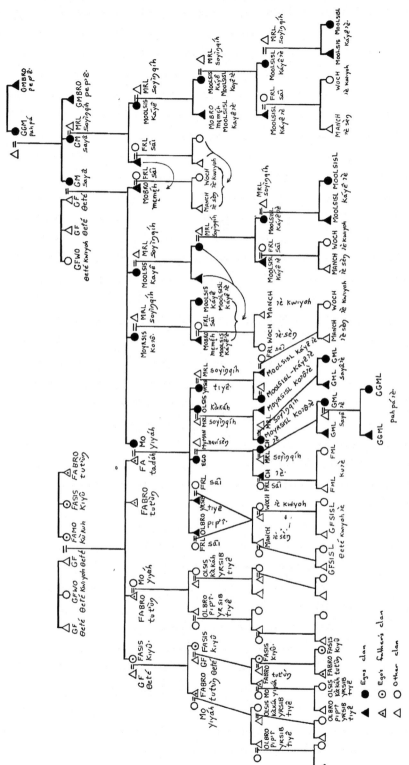

Fig. 2. Hopi-Tewa kinship system—female ego.

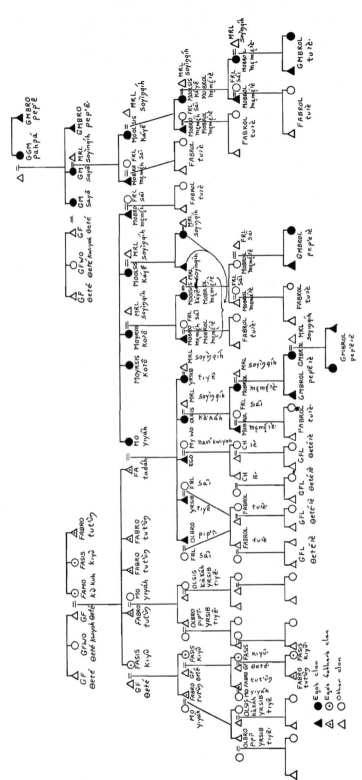

Fig. 3. Hopi-Tewa kinship system—male ego.

mother's brother, who are called *pep'ê·*. A man calls each of his own children *è·*,[4] child; each of his children's children and his brother's children's children, *θété?è·*, mother's or father's father (diminutive).[5] All junior members of the lineage he calls by the junior reciprocal *mɛmɛ́?è·*, mother's brother (diminutive), except for his grandnephews and great-grandnephews, whom he calls *pép'ê?è·*, mother's mother's brother (diminutive).

In speaking of persons in her generation and above, a woman makes the same distinctions as the man for her relatives in the lineage. Below her generation in the lineage, a woman distinguishes her own children as *?è·*, child; her daughter's children as *sáyâ?è·*, mother's mother (diminutive); and her daughter's daughter's children as *páhpâ?è·*, mother's mother's mother (diminutive). A woman differentiates her younger sister's children *káyê·?è·*, mother's older sister (diminutive); and her older sister's children *kó?ô?è·*, mother's younger sister (diminutive). A woman's older and younger sister's daughter's children are classified together as *sáyâ?è·*, mother's mother (diminutive).

A man calls his younger and older brother's children *tu?è·*, father's brother (diminutive), and uses the same term for all children of men of his lineage. Younger and older brother's children's children are called *θété·?è·*, mother's or father's father (diminutive).

In the father's matrilineal lineage all men except father (*tádah*) are called *tut'ùŋ*,[6] father's brother; all women are called *kiyû*, father's sister, except the father's mother, who is called *kù·kuh*.[7] All men marrying women of father's lineage are called *θeté·*, mother's or father's father; and all women marrying men of father's lineage are called *yiyah*, mother. Male children of men of father's lineage are called *píp'î*, older brother, and *tíyê·*, younger sibling. Female children of men of father's lineage are called *kà·káh*, older sister, and *tíyê·*, younger sibling.

All men of mother's father's lineage and father's father's lineage are classed together as *θeté·*, mother's or father's father; and all women of these lineages are classed together as *θeté·kʷíyoh*, mother's or father's father woman.

Men marrying women of ego's lineage are called *soyìŋgíh*, male relative-in-law; women marrying men of ego's lineage are called *sa'*, female relative-in-law. These individuals call ego, if male, *yaséno*, in-law-man; if female, *yakʷíyoh*, in-law-woman.

A child of a man of the lineage is called *?è·*, child, male speaking; or *?è·sèŋ*, male child, and *?è·kʷíyoh*, female child, female speaking.

Hopi-Tewa kinship terms are the same or obviously cognate with those of the Rio Grande Tewa.[8] Like the Rio Grande Tewa, siblings and mother's sisters are distinguished on the basis of seniority. The junior reciprocal, as among the Rio Grande Tewa, is used extensively. In spite of these similarities to the Rio Grande Tewa

---

[4] All kinship terms are given in singular form—*?è·*, child; but *?ê·*, children.

[5] "Diminutive" refers to the junior reciprocal, that is, every relationship term has a reciprocal diminutive form, applied by a senior to a junior member of the society. This is achieved by the addition of *?è·*, child, to the senior form: thus; *mɛmɛ́h*, uncle, and *mɛmɛ́?è·*, uncle child, or little uncle (nephew).

[6] Eggan (1950, pp. 141–144) uses the term *tádah*, father (cf. Barbara Freire-Marreco, 1914, pp. 268–287). I have found *tut'ùŋ*, father's brother, to be used most frequently instead.

[7] This term is applied to any woman of father's clan who cuts the umbilical cord at birth—it is usually the father's mother, but in her absence one of father's sisters may perform the function.

[8] For Rio Grande Tewa relationship terms see Harrington, 1912, pp. 472–498.

kinship system, Hopi-Tewa kinship structure differs hardly at all from the Hopi.[9] The system, like that of the Hopi, is organized on a lineage principle, quite different from the bilateral, generational type of the Rio Grande Tewa. The kinship charts (figs. 2 and 3) show clearly the importance of the matrilineal lineage. Correspondingly, behavioral patterns are consonant with the lineage and household structures (see below). Thus the Hopi-Tewa kinship system seems to have been reorganized along the Hopi pattern without the terms themselves being greatly modified.[10]

EXTENSION OF TERMS

There is a wide range of individuals to whom kinship terms are extended. Extension of terms embraces lineage, clan, and, in certain cases, linked clans of the Hopi, the Navaho, and the Rio Grande Pueblo Indians.

The term *káyê·*, mother's older sister, is a general term for all senior women of one's clan. Younger women are called by the junior reciprocal *káyê·ʔè·*, mother's older sister (diminutive). Very old women are called *sayâ·*. mother's mother.

All older men of one's own clan are called *mεmέh*, mother's brother; and its junior reciprocal, *mεmε?è·*, mother's brother (diminutive) is applied to all very young members of the clan.

The terms given above are applied to all equivalent Hopi, Navaho, and Rio Grande pueblo clans. Rio Grande Tewa, regardless of clan affiliation, are called by clan terms as if they were of the same clan. For showing respect to Rio Grande Tewa individuals, the senior terms are employed even though the person addressed may be considerably younger. Thus, when a group of Hopi-Tewa were visiting Santa Clara Pueblo in the winter of 1950 the visitors all called my sister *káyê·*, although she was younger than most of the Hopi-Tewa. They also used the term *mεmέh* for adults obviously younger than themselves. Only for children were the junior reciprocals used. At Tewa Village I was called *mεmέh* by the very old as well as by the very young.

Four categories of ceremonial sponsors[11] exist: (1) A ceremonial father is selected for a boy between the ages of eight and ten, and a ceremonial mother for a girl of similar age, when the boy or girl enters the katcina cult. (2) A ceremonial father inducts a young man into the Winter Solstice ceremony when he is between twelve and sixteen years old.[12] (3) A "doctor father"[13] is selected for a man or boy who is very ill (a "doctor mother," for a woman or girl); he is supposed to cure the patient, who is given to him in "adoption." (4) A ceremonial sponsor—a man for a boy and a

---

[9] Eggan (1950, pp. 23, 24, 142, 143) has shown the similarity of Hopi and Hopi-Tewa kinship structures by a series of lineage diagrams.

[10] Eggan (1950, p. 156) suggests that changes in kinship behavior, associated with the adoption of the Hopi household-lineage-clan pattern, are the major causes of the reorganization of the kinship system.

The fact that the Hopi-Tewa terms have remained unchanged is interesting in terms of the speculations about the determinants of kinship terminology. For an exhaustive review and discussion of this subject, see Murdock, 1949, pp. 113–183.

[11] See "The Life Cycle," below, for a detailed discussion of ceremonial sponsors.

[12] The Winter Solstice ceremonial father may be the same as the katcina-initiation sponsor, but ordinarily another man is chosen. Women are not inducted into this ceremony; at a comparable age, however, they grind corn for four days and have their hair style changed to "cart wheels." In this duty, girls are assisted by their father's sisters and women of father's clan. See pp. 317, 328.

[13] This person is not necessarily a curer but one who is respected in the community. His function as a "doctor father" or "doctor mother" is to "hold good thoughts" for the patient and thereby help him get well.

woman for a girl—is selected for a young person about to become a member of a curing society.

The ceremonial sponsor must be from a clan other than that of the novice, but may be of the novice's father's clan. The Hopi-Tewa believe that a novice becomes a member of his (or her) sponsor's clan, and clan kinship terms are extended to embrace the sponsor's clan and phratry. The relations between a novice and his ceremonial sponsor are, however, much more affectionate than between members of the same clan. The relations that exist between the sponsor and the novice are more like those between father and son or between father's sister and her brother's daughter.[14] Indeed, the terms "father" and "mother" are used by a man and woman respectively in addressing a ceremonial sponsor, although clan relationship terms are used for other members of the sponsor's clan.

There is no restriction of marriage between ego and members of his ceremonial sponsor's clan. He is forbidden to marry (1) a member of the same clan or phratry or a member of an equivalent Hopi, Rio Grande pueblo, or Navaho clan; (2) a member of father's clan or its linked clans; and (3) a person whose father's clan is the same as ego's.

Although a man's (or woman's) ties are closest within his own clan, marriage, ceremonial sponsors, and affiliation with equivalent clans and phratries of Hopi and other tribes extend his relationships considerably beyond his own clan. These social mechanisms afford security to the individual and provide for social, ceremonial, and economic interaction with a wide range of individuals. The privileges and responsibilities involved in the extended kinship system are thus important for individual and group satisfactions.[15]

THE HOUSEHOLD

Before kinship behavior is discussed, the extended matrilineal household,[16] where an individual receives his initial and basic cultural orientation, should be thoroughly understood. This unit is extremely important, even though, like the Hopi, the Hopi-Tewa do not formally recognize it (see Eggan, 1950, p. 50; Titiev, 1944, pp. 8–10). The household normally consists of a woman and her husband, married daughters and their husbands, unmarried sons, and children of the daughters. The women comprise the important part of the unit—they own the house, dispense foodstuffs, and care for the religious paraphernalia. The oldest woman of the household enjoys the most respect, and the members of the unit look to her for instructions and seek her advice in times of trouble. Next in importance is her oldest daughter, who assumes the duties and responsibilities of the household in the absence of her mother. Men of the household and lineage leave the house when they marry, although they return frequently, consider it their home, exercise considerable authority in religious matters, and are called to exert discipline over the children in serious cases. The husbands have little authority in the wife's home; they contribute to its economic support, teach their children "how to make a living," and provide warmth and real affection toward them but defer to their wives and their wives' brothers and uncles in disciplinary matters.

---

[14] See "Kinship Behavior," below.

[15] *Ibid.*

[16] Freire-Marreco (1914, pp. 281–283) has given an excellent description of the Hopi-Tewa household as it existed forty years ago. Eggan (1950, p. 156) considers the Hopi-Tewa household as described by Freire-Marreco to be almost an exact duplicate of the Hopi household.

Formerly, the extended household occupied a series of adjacent rooms. With the increasing importance of wage work and livestock activities in recent years, this situation has changed. Hopi-Tewa families on farms and ranches during the summer are essentially of the nucelar-family type: husband, wife, and children—and in some cases a widowed grandmother, a divorced daughter, or other relative and her children—are present. For wage workers, housing limitations at Keams Canyon or off the reservation restrict the size of the household even more drastically.[17] Although it is not uncommon to have one or even both parents of the wife living with a nuclear family on a farm or ranch, older people refuse to make their home with children who live in government quarters or off the reservation.

At Polacca and Tewa Village the size and composition of the households varies seasonally and with the occurrence of ceremonial and social functions. During these events the households are considerably larger. Hopi-Tewa members consider the residences on farms or ranches, at Keams Canyon, or off the reservation as temporary and retain homes at Tewa Village or Polacca. Here they return frequently for various social and ceremonial occasions and revert to extended-household living.[18]

The household in recent years has thus tended to become a less integrated unit than it was formerly; nevertheless there is keen awareness of all the relatives that comprise the household group. Modern forms of transportation afford frequent resumptions of extended-household living. The growing child still has a maximum of contact with a large number of relatives. A child soon learns to identify grandparents, parents, his mother's sisters and their husbands and children, and his own brothers and sisters. For much of the time he eats, sleeps, and plays in the company of these relatives.

Almost simultaneously with his contact with the relatives of the household group, though not with the same frequency, the child comes into contact with his father's relatives. These relatives, particularly father's mother and father's sisters, are frequent visitors to his house, and he is always welcome and treated with affection in their house. At crucial periods of his life they comfort and aid him. Thus, for example, when the Soyoku come at the time of the Powamu ceremony, these relatives intercede for him and prevent the frightening ogres from carrying him away.[19]

The enculturation process will become more evident in the discussion of kinship behavior and the life cycle, but the initial indoctrination of a Hopi-Tewa individual cannot be thoroughly understood unless the importance of the structural make-up of the household is comprehended.

KINSHIP BEHAVIOR

My observations of Hopi-Tewa kinship behavior are essentially parallel to those reported by Titiev (1944, pp. 15–29) and Eggan (1950, pp. 31–42) for the Hopi. I have noted where differences occur, but such deviations appear to be minor and

---

[17] Government housing is extremely poor, often consisting of only a flimsy one- or two-room frame house. The size of these quarters is often smaller than mesa-top homes, and the construction is inferior; moreover, agency officials object to more than one nuclear family occupying a government house.

[18] The extended household described in detail with relation to economic activities in chap. v, under "Sharing within the Household," may be taken as an example of a typical Hopi-Tewa household. The highly mobile and segmenting quality of the household is also apparent in the illustration.

[19] See below, under "Social Control," for a description of the Soyoku and an account of their annual visits.

perhaps are explainable in terms of Tewa or Tano ancestry. Apparently by virtue of a long period of intermarriage, kinship behavior has come to approximate Hopi patterns.

In illustrating kinship behavior I shall draw mainly from the extended household in which I made my residence in the initial phases of my research. From comparative observations of other Hopi-Tewa households, that of my hosts appeared to be typical. I feel, therefore, that observational data from this household group are valid for a characterization of kinship behavior of the Hopi-Tewa generally.

Father ⟵⟶ Son
tádah ⟵⟶ ʔèˑ

Father, *tádah* (a man of about sixty), and son *ʔèˑ* (a man of about twenty-six), habitually worked together. They farmed, herded sheep and cattle, mended corral fences, butchered livestock, and performed a host of other tasks. Both performed most of the jobs well, and each worked independently. In activities new or unfamiliar to *ʔèˑ*, however, he watched his father carefully and then repeated the task, often with kindly words of instruction from *tádah*. I did not see *ʔèˑ* punished or reprimanded by his father during my stay in the household.

In the winter of 1951, *ʔèˑ* injured himself by falling off the mesa cliff when he was intoxicated. When he recovered after a long sojourn in the hospital, his mother, *yáyah*, and her brother, *mɛmɛ́h* (terms as used by *ʔèˑ*), severely reprimanded him for drinking and exacted a promise from him to desist from it. As the two were scolding him, *tádah* stood beside *ʔèˑ*, enjoining leniency.

On many occasions *ʔèˑ* bought tobacco in the local trading post and presented it to *tádah* without being asked; *tádah* also performed such favors for *ʔèˑ*. Under all circumstances the behavior was mutually one of deep attachment.

Father ⟵⟶ Daughter
tádah ⟵⟶ ʔèˑ

tádah and daughter *ʔèˑ* (a nineteen-year-old girl) show considerable affection for one another. *ʔèˑ* often sits by *tádah* at the table, and *tádah* passes choice bits of food to her. Often *ʔèˑ* rests her head on *tádah*'s shoulder while he gently pats her head.

On one occasion *ʔèˑ* lost a ten-dollar bill her father had given her to buy some clothes in the trading post. *yíyah* scolded her for being careless and told her she would not get any money from her. When *yíyah* turned her back and walked into the next room, *tádah* brought out a five-dollar bill and quietly gave it to *ʔèˑ*. Daughter's eyes filled with tears, and she pressed her father's hand affectionately.

When *ʔèˑ* wanted to go to the Mission school, it was *tádah* who decided the issue. *yíyah* did not want her to go, and though her daughter had not talked with *tádah* about it before, she suddenly turned in the midst of a heated argument and asked him: "*tádah*, you think it is all right for me to go, don't you?" *tádah* nodded his head affirmatively and then proceeded to side with his daughter in the discussion. *yíyah* was finally won over.

In a store in Gallup, *ʔèˑ* once picked out a shirt for her father and made *mɛmɛ́h* buy it for her. On the same trip, *tádah* bought for his daughter several articles of clothing, which he kept secret from her until they had returned home, much to the delight of *ʔèˑ*.

A father's extremely affectionate regard for his children may be in part prompted by a desire to entrench himself in the household in which he is an outsider. A wife's and her children's loyalties are primarily with their own lineage and clan; conversely, a husband is committed to his own lineage and clan. Through the custom of matrilocal residence and duties to his wife and children, however, he has responsibilities for supporting the whole household (with the aid of unmarried men of his wife's household and the men married into it). These conflicting roles make his position insecure and the marriage bond rather unstable.[20] The affectionate tie between a father and his children helps cement his position in the household. Children, because of the warm regard they have for their father, will often arbitrate controversies and effect compromises between father and mother. I have also observed on several occasions *ʔê·* (son and daughter) praising the work of their father in the hearing of *yíyah* (mother) and *mɛmɛ́h* (mother's brother). "*tádah* did more work than all of us" is a phrase I have often heard *ʔè·* (son) make after returning from a task in which all the men of the household had worked.

Father's Brother ⟵⟶ Brother's Son, Daughter

tut'ùŋ ⟵—————————⟶ *tuʔè·*

Although the father's brother is sometimes called *tádah*, father, he is most often *tut'ùŋ*, father's brother. The reciprocal term used by *tut'ùŋ* is *tuʔè·*, father's brother (diminutive).

Eggan (1950, pp. 32–33) reports that the Hopi normally make little distinction between father and father's brother. The father used in the previous example did not have a brother living, and I did not have an opportunity to observe the relationship in another household. I asked the senior woman of the household in which I resided to explain the relationship, however. She reported:

> Our *tut'ùŋ* helps us in many ways, and we always feel welcome in his house, but he is not our father. Our father lives with us all the time and he works for us and buys things for us. Sometimes we will help our *tut'ùŋ* because *tádah* has asked us to do so and we always want to please our *tádah*. When we go to *tut'ùŋ*'s house he treats us kindly, but he has his own wife and children to support and he cannot give us many things. In Tewa we call him *tádah*, father, out of respect when we talk to him, just like we also call the Village Chief *tádah* to his face, but we know that he is not really our *tádah*.

This woman's knowledge of Hopi-Tewa customs is unusually profound, and her information is generally accurate. It would seem from her remarks, then, that the Hopi-Tewa, unlike the Hopi, make a sharp distinction between the real father and father's brother.

Mother ⟵⟶ Son

yíyah ⟵—————⟶ *ʔè·*

Mother, *yíyah*, is about sixty years old. She is the wife of *tádah*; *ʔè·* is their son. Both *tádah* and *ʔè·* have been considered previously in the father-son relationship. We have already seen that *yíyah* reprimanded her son when *ʔè·* returned from the hospital. I have heard *yíyah* scold her son on many other occasions as well, particularly with reference to his drinking.

---

[20] Similar characterizations of Hopi marriage relationship are to be found in Eggan, 1950, pp. 34–35; Titiev, 1944, pp. 39–43. Marital breakups among the Hopi-Tewa, however, are not as frequent as at Oraibi, where almost 40 per cent of the marriages end in divorce (Titiev, 1944, p. 39). The Hopi-Tewa divorce rate is about 20 per cent (see n. 22, below).

ʔèˑ has always wanted a pickup truck, and he has often talked about this with other members of the household. *yíyah* is strongly opposed to getting a car. "You will only wreck it and kill yourself," she told him one day. This started an argument between them. ʔèˑ talked in low tones and tried to convince his mother that he would be very careful with the truck. But *yíyah* raised her voice and told ʔèˑ why she was opposed. Most of her reasons involved his drinking and the danger of wrecking the car and injuring himself and others. As she was talking, her brother, *mɛmɛ́h* (ʔèˑ speaking), entered, and he joined the discussion, supporting his sister. While the argument was going on, *tádah* entered the room and quietly spoke to his wife: "People outside will hear." Whereupon all three stopped talking immediately, and the subject was not brought up the rest of the day.

There is genuine affection between *yíyah* and ʔèˑ, but it is not manifested in the same manner as between *tádah* and ʔèˑ Neither does *yíyah* speak softly and affectionately to her son as does *tádah*'s sister to ʔèˑ Yet when ʔèˑ was injured, she arranged for her son to be carried to the hospital at Keams Canyon and went along herself. After ʔèˑ was examined, she prodded the doctor and nurses for information about his condition, unashamed of her broken English in this crisis situation. ʔèˑ was transferred to the Fort Defiance hospital, and *yíyah* and *tádah* went along. They lived and boarded with a Navaho family and kept a daily vigil by their son's bedside until he was released a month later.

According to informants, the mother-son relationship is deep and enduring. Even after a son leaves home at marriage, he frequently returns for aid and advice. A mother may scold and admonish her son, but this is her right as a mother, and the son is not ordinarily much disturbed by her anger. Serious advice and admonition are usually referred to the mother's brother, the disciplinarian of the household. A mother has the primary decision in the selection of her son's "ceremonial father" and gives the man who is chosen food and gifts in recompense for his services.

A son has deep affection for his mother and performs many services and favors for her. The report of an old Hopi-Tewa woman, generalizing about children, is worth quoting here:

"We prefer daughters to sons because daughters we have with us always and they bring us men [through marriage] to help us make a living. Sons we only raise for other families, and a woman with only sons is poor indeed. Yet a son is always prized, for he is kind and gentle. He will often gladden the heart of a mother with a gift even though he has long since moved to another house and has a family of his own."

Mother ⟷ Daughter

yíyah ⟷ ʔèˑ

The relation between *yíyah* mother (used in the above illustration) and ʔèˑ daughter (also considered above) is not typical, because of ʔèˑ's schooling experiences and the discrepancy in ages. I have described the mother's reaction to her daughter in chapter ii. Since the parent-children relationship, particularly, is being influenced and changed by modern conditions, however, it would perhaps be well to keep the account in mind.

According to many Hopi-Tewa with whom I discussed the mother-daughter relationship, the mother trains the daughter in all domestic duties: grinding corn, cooking, taking care of babies, and the like. A mother and daughter constantly confide in one another. At least in the recent past, a daughter immediately informed her mother of her first menstruation; her mother then took her to the girl's father's sister's house, and she underwent the puberty ceremony there (see "The Life Cycle," below). Important ritual knowledge pertaining to the clan is transmitted from mother to daughter. A daughter has the deepest affection for her mother and constantly aspires to be like her.

The foregoing appears to be the actual behavior except in a few isolated instances in which modern pressures have produced a rift between parents and children. In such families are the "bad" and "mean" children who are disrespectful to the old people and are averse to participating in traditional activities and ceremonies.

Mother's Older Sister ⟷ Younger Sister's Son, Daughter

káyê· ⟵——————————————⟶ káyê·ʔè·

The relation between *káyê·* (mother's older sister) and her younger sister's children, *káyê·ʔè·*, is different from that between *kóʔô·* (mother's younger sister) and the latter's older sister's children. *káyê·* demands more aid and gives more orders to her younger sister's children. In return *káyê·* receives strict obedience from them. A younger sister often sends her children to be admonished or instructed in certain domestic and ritual duties by her older sister. This is particularly true if both *sayâ·* (mother's mother) and *sayâ·*'s sister (also called *sayâ·*) are absent.

yíyah (mother used in the previous examples) has an older sister about sixty-eight years old. Just a few days before a katcina dance in the summer of 1951, *yíyah* sent her daughter to the household piki house, where *káyê·* was making piki. *yíyah* had arranged beforehand with her older sister to have her daughter instructed. *káyê·* greeted her niece affectionately when she came and asked her to sit by her side and watch her work. As *káyê·* worked, she spoke gently to her niece, *káyê·ʔè·*, explaining the details of making the thin, paper-like sheets of corn-meal bread. She demonstrated the exact portions of batter to pick up on her finger tips and told her to be careful to run her hands swiftly over the heated flat rock when she spread the batter. After a considerable period of demonstration, *káyê·* permitted her niece to take her position. *káyê·* was patient and gentle in her instructions as she carefully observed and gently criticized her niece's work. When the instruction period was over, *káyê·* complimented her niece and said that she was convinced *káyê·ʔè·* would become a fine piki maker.

Relations between *káyê·* and her younger sister's son, *káyê·ʔè·*, are marked by the same affection and gentleness. Contacts between these two relatives are less frequent, because of the difference in sex, but the relations that exist are mutually affectionate.

The position of *káyê·* is superseded only by *sayâ·* (mother's mother) in the household. She has a great deal to say about both the store of foodstuffs and ritual matters. As *sayâ·* becomes old and less able to perform her duties, *káyê·* takes on more and more authority. Freire-Marreco noted also the special position of *káyê·*. The following is expressed in the words of a hypothetical Tewa girl, a unique and effective method used to illustrate kinship behavior (Freire-Marreco, 1914, p. 282):

"My eldest *kóʔô·* generally called *naví*[21] *káyê·* partakes somewhat of *sayâ·*'s

---

[21] *naví* (my or mine) is used for emphasis in front of a kinship term. It is generally omitted in habitual conversation. The phonetic symbols used in this quotation have been adjusted to my own system of orthography.

authority, gives out stores in her absence, buys and sells corn and meat, and knows where the masks are kept."

Mother's Younger Sister ⟷ Older Sister's Son, Daughter
kóʔô· ⟵⟶ *kóʔô·ʔè·*

kóʔô· is the term used for mother's younger sister; the reciprocal is *kóʔô·ʔè·*. This relationship was illustrated by *káyê·*'s (*yíyah*'s older sister), two grown daughters, and *yíyah. káyê·*'s daughters respect *kóʔô·*, but the deep respect accorded to a *káyê·* is not present in their behavior. Rather they behave toward *kóʔô·* as if she were merely an older sister, *kà·káh*. A mild form of joking between them was also noted on several occasions. When I asked *káyô·*'s oldest daughter to let me take a photograph of her nine-year-old daughter in the "cart-wheel" hairdress worn by girls after puberty, she called her *kóʔô·* to dress her daughter's hair. As *kóʔô·* worked, *káyê·*'s daughters joked with her mildly. They said *kóʔô·* was slow and that she ought to work faster. If *kóʔô·* pulled on the hair too hard, they laughed, much to the annoyance of both *kóʔô·* and her grandniece. *kóʔô·* remonstrated with her older sister's daughters, telling them that they were just like the girls of the younger generation, ignorant of traditional tasks, even a simple one such as dressing a girl's hair.

A *kóʔô·*'s behavior toward her older sister's sons is also informal, but no joking goes on between them.

Behavioral patterns among the Hopi-Tewa are to a large extent determined by relative age. If a mother's sister is much older than her nieces and nephews though younger than their mother, she is still likely to be shown considerable respect. In the case mentioned above, the discrepancy in ages between *kóʔô·* and her older sister's daughters is not very great. *kóʔô·* is therefore more like an older sister to *káyê·*'s daughters. Behavior is also influenced by the kind of relations that exist between a parent and the relative under consideration. *káyê·*, for example tends to joke with her younger sister and order her around, and thus influences the behavior of her own daughters toward their *kóʔô·*.

From the preceding illustrations it will be seen that a son's or daughter's relations with a mother's older sister are distinctly different from those that exist between such children and a mother's younger sister. Relations between a woman and her sisters' children are also different from those that exist between a woman and her own children. This, too, is evident from the previous illustrations. Eggan (1950, p. 33) remarks that the position of mother's sister among the Hopi is practically identical with that of the mother; the Hopi-Tewa do not share this trait with their Hopi neighbors.

Husband ⟷ Wife
sèŋ ⟵⟶ *kʷíyoh*

tádah and *yíyah*, considered separately in the preceding illustrations, are *sèŋ* and *kʷíyoh*, husband and wife. They are very much devoted to each other, but they never openly demonstrate their affection. I have, for instance, never seen one touch the other, or noted any form of tender gesture between them to indicate their affection for one another. There are, however, subtle signs indicative of warm regard. When one talks to the other, a gentleness creeps into the voice. *sèŋ* has on many occasions demonstrated his regard for *kʷíyoh* by buying utilitarian but nonessential items for his wife. *kᵂtyoh* performs little services for *sèŋ*, such as caring for his clothing and combing his hair. They are often together, going to the spring, to the corrals, or to the trading post. *kᵂtyoh* and *sèŋ* do not walk side by side—he is usually two paces in front while she trudges behind, which is the Hopi and Hopi-Tewa manner for a husband and wife to walk and is not indicative of subordinate or superordinate relationship.

Hopi-Tewa marriages appear to be set in firmer foundations than Hopi ones, at least when compared with Oraibi. The divorce rate for Oraibi is almost 40 per cent; for the Hopi-Tewa it is about half that.[22]

There is a great deal of affection and coöperation in performing the duties of everyday life. A man has economic obligations to his wife, and together with others is responsible for the support of her household. She in turn extends hospitality to, and prepares food for, his guests on feast days and other occasions.

In the event of separation and divorce, the husband returns to his mother's home and there resumes a life very much like the one he led before he was married. The extended family structure in the divorced wife's household cushions the loss of the husband; children and wife do not feel the loss of a husband and father as keenly as in societies lacking such kinship devices.[23]

Mother's Brother ⟵⟶ Sister's Children

mɛmɛ́h ⟵⟶ *mɛmɛ?ê·*

One of the most important of Hopi-Tewa kinship relationships is that of a man to his sister's children. The mother's brother is chief disciplinarian to his sister's children, and they both respect and obey him. Usually the sister's oldest brother takes the role, but in his absence a mother's younger brother may be called to perform the function of disciplining his sister's children.[24] The mother's brother is generally feared by the children, and often the mere mention of his name, with a threat to call him if the children do not behave, is enough to make them conform. Mother's oldest brother (if mother's mother's brother is not alive) is frequently important as the ritual head of the clan. He and mother are responsible for clan rituals and often get together to discuss such affairs.

An illustration of *mɛmɛ́h*'s anger toward his sister's son, *mɛmɛ?è*, has already been noted.[25] In certain respects the behavior of *mɛmɛ́h* to his sister's children is like that of *yíyah* to her own children. When I was living in the household I frequently heard mother's brother speak to his sister's children, but his voice was characteristically without warmth. *mɛmɛ́h*, like *yíyah*, seemed always to be ordering or admonishing his sister's children. Yet *mɛmɛ́h* has deep regard for his nephews and nieces. When his nephew was in the hospital at Fort Defiance as a result of the injury I have already reported, I visited *mɛmɛ?è·* (nephew) several times. When I returned to the household after such trips, *mɛmɛ́h* was always the first to greet me, inquiring about news of his nephew. The youth had fractured his skull and was in an un-

---

[22] Of 144 married Hopi-Tewa, only 23 have been divorced previously. For Oraibi divorce rates, see Titiev, 1944, pp. 34–35.

[23] Especially since the father usually continues to live in the same village and still has frequent contact with his children.

[24] Discipline is never corporal. Scoldings and threats of supernatural intervention (e.g., disobedience might bring on a dire famine or epidemic) are the common forms of discipline.

[25] See "Father⟵⟶Son," above.

conscious state for more than a week. The surgeon had to perform a delicate operation, which fortunately was successful. After returning from my first visit to the hospital, I gave *mɛmɛ́h* a detailed report of the operation. As I spoke, his eyes filled with tears, and at the end of my account he cried. Yet when *mɛmɛ́ʔè·* (nephew) returned from the hospital, *mɛmɛ́h* and *yíyah* reprimanded him severely.

A child has deep respect for his mother's brother, though he may fear him. The child obeys him and listens attentively to his instructions, particularly with reference to ritual affairs. As a son or daughter grows up, *mɛmɛ́h* becomes more of a confidant and a source of information, while his disciplinary functions diminish. It is true that *mɛmɛ́h* is sometimes called to settle marital quarrels and to warn a young man not to drink; but this is infrequent, as adults are expected to behave properly and generally do so.

Older Brother ⟷ Younger Brother

pɪp'i· ⟵————————⟶ *tiyê·*

Brothers coöperate closely, and the coöperation may continue even after marriage. In spite of their living in separate households, brothers usually herd sheep and cattle together. Common participation in ceremonies generally continues after marriage.

Actually observed behavior may be illustrated from the A—— lineage, in which there are several brothers. Three of the brothers are married and live with their families in separate households. These brothers pool their cattle herds and work together in herding, branding, butchering, and other ranching activities. Four of the brothers are unmarried and live with their widowed mother, two married sisters, and the sisters' husbands and children. These young boys—aged about fifteen to twenty—work with the husbands of their sisters on the farm plots of their mother's clan lands. Periodically they also help their older brothers in their livestock activities. All seven brothers are active in the ceremonial affairs of the Central Plaza Kiva and take a lively part in the annual katcina cycle. Two of the unmarried brothers love to dance and are usually active in the small social group dances held in January.[26]

It was reported that one of the married brothers once accused a younger brother of making advances toward his wife, and told this younger brother to keep away from his wife and his house. For a long time hostile feelings existed between these two brothers. The younger brother has since married and now has several children. Apparently the ill feeling between the two brothers has been forgotten, for they now help each other in ranching activities and coöperate in ceremonial functions.

Hostility between brothers was reported to exist in other households, but I did not personally know of another case. The A—— brothers appear to get along remarkably well—they coöperate in all major activities and are manifestly devoted to one another.

Deference from a younger to an older brother is a common form of behavior. An older brother has the right, according to Hopi-Tewa belief, to order, chastise, and demand obedience from a younger brother. This is a privilege that is often exercised, and the younger brother obeys and listens attentively to an older one's remonstrances. The older brother is also conceived of as the guardian of his younger

---

[26] See "Ritual Activities Today," in chap. iv., for an account of social group dances.

siblings and is supposed to watch that they do not get injured or fall into mischief. When a younger sibling is hurt or gets into trouble, it is often said that it happened because the older brother was not attentive. If the discrepancy in age between a younger and an older brother is very great, the older brother may, in fact, take a position almost like that of *memeh*, mother's brother. This is particularly true in families that have no mother's brother.

Older Sister ⟵⟶ Younger Sister

kà·kâh ⟵—————⟶ *tiyê·*

The relation of sisters to one another is very intimate and lifelong. Sisters rear and care for their children in the same household and coöperate in all household tasks.[27] An older sister may often assume an importance equal to that of the mother in the household, particularly if she is the oldest daughter in the household and the other children are considerably younger than she. There is in Hopi-Tewa a special term, *kà·kâh*, to distinguish older sister from *tiyê·*, younger sibling.

In the household of my hosts, the three daughters of one of the women were respectively nine, ten, and sixteen years old. The two younger sisters went to school, played, and worked together. Sometimes they quarreled or fought over the possession of some toy. Their mother often called on her oldest daughter to settle the argument: "Tell *A* to stop picking on her younger sister *B*!" The oldest sister would then arbitrate, emphasizing that they must mind her because she is older, and that *A* should be ashamed for permitting a quarrel, because she is older than *B* and should know better. This reasoning was usually effective in stopping arguments between the two younger sisters.

Age difference between adult sisters with respect to their children's behavior toward them has already been described. Relative age is thus extremely important in terms of social control and general behavior in the household.

Brother ⟵⟶ Sister

pip'i· ⟵—⟶ *tiyê·*

Although all those I asked agreed that the term *tiyê·* referred to younger sibling, yet the girls and women in the household always called a brother *pip'i·*, older brother, even though he was younger than the speaker. Similarly, brothers generally referred to their sisters as *tiyê·*, younger sibling, regardless of age. Freire-Marreco (1914, p. 276) also noted this usage; she reports:

"Apart from the question of relative age, brothers in general are *pip'i·*, sisters *tiyê·*;[28] it seems that brothers are assumed to be senior to sisters, and entitled to respect as such, in the absence of evidence to the contrary."

This distinction and the importance generally given to seniority probably reflect a retention of Rio Grande Tewa kinship usage. Among these Tewa, considerable emphasis is given to relative age, and male dominance is evident in certain patterns, such as the greater importance of the father in the household and male ownership of houses and land.[29]

---

[27] This practice is becoming less common in recent years because of the periodic segmentations of the Hopi-Tewa households.

[28] Phonetics have been adjusted to my orthography.

[29] Ethnographic notes on Santa Clara Pueblo.

The actual behavior between brother and sister does not reveal patterns of subordination and superordination, however. There is a great deal of coöperation and exchange of confidences between brother and sister. Even though a brother and sister are eventually separated by marriage and subsequent residence in different households, contact is still maintained. A sister often advises a brother about making a proper marriage, and frequently has much to say about whom her brother should marry. Sisters aid in the preparation of food on ceremonial occasions in which their brother participates.

The behavior described above was illustrated by the daughter and son of *yíyah* (who has previously been considered in other relationships). Sister, *tiyê·*, showed extreme affection and respect for her brother, *pîp'î·*, and she often asked about his girl friends, giving expression of her approval or censorship of these girls. When *pîp'î·* started to go with a certain girl and then decided to marry her, *tiyê·* objected and pointed out with great emotion the flaws in this girl's character. *pîp'î·* married the girl in spite of his sister's disapproval; but apparently his sister's objections made an impression, for he separated from his wife within a week and returned to his natal household. Eventually he secured a divorce, and his life in his sister's and mother's household was marred by only a week's absence.

Although paternal parallel cousins are also called brothers and sisters—*kà·kâh*, *pîp'î·*, and *tiyê·*—the relationship is not intimate. Interaction is infrequent, since they live in separate households.

Maternal Parallel Cousins

$$m\varepsilon m\acute{\varepsilon} h \longleftrightarrow m\varepsilon m\varepsilon ?\grave{e}·$$
$$k\acute{o}?\acute{o}· \longleftrightarrow k\acute{o}?\acute{o}·?\grave{e}·$$

The behavior of maternal parallel cousins toward each other is comparable to that between siblings. Relative age is important, behavior and terms being adjusted accordingly. Thus, mother's sister's son if older than male or female ego is called *mεmέh*; if younger, he is called *mεmε?è·* by male ego and *kó?ó·è·* by female ego. Mother's sister's daughter if older than male or female ego is called *kó?ó·*; if younger, she is called *mεmέ?è·* by male ego and *kó?ó·?è·* by female ego. Greater respect and obedience is accorded an older maternal parallel cousin.

Since relatives ordinarily live together or in close proximity, the relations are frequent, intimate, and marked with deep attachment. In recent years, modern conditions have tended to limit the interaction of maternal parallel cousins by the necessary divisions of the extended household, but these relatives still come together frequently at social and ceremonial functions.

Father's Sister ⟷ Brother's Son

$$kiy\hat{u}· \longleftrightarrow ?\grave{e}·s\grave{e}\eta$$

An extremely affectionate relationship exists between father's sister, *kiyû·*, and her brother's son, *?è·sèŋ*. Father's sisters manifest a deep interest in their *?è·sèŋ* from the time of his birth (see "The Life Cycle," below) and continue a warm relationship for life. Usually a father's sister takes upon herself to become the special guardian of one of her brother's sons. Other women of father's clan may select other sons of their clansbrother on whom to bestow special attention and affection. Such a father's clanswoman appears in her brother's house at crucial periods of her brother's son's life. If he has been injured or is ill, *kiyû·* will come immediately to console and comfort her *ʔèˑsèŋ*. When the ogres come on the morning before Powamu she is at her brother's house to "protect" her *ʔèˑsèŋ* from the child's own clansfolk, who "pretend to give away the child" to these frightful-appearing katcinas.[30] As the boy becomes older, *kiyû·* "pretends to be jealous" of her *ʔèˑsèŋ*'s regard for his girl friends.

During a buffalo dance in January, 1951, two girls and two boys danced in the middle of the village courtyard. A woman spectator suddenly ran out among the dancers, pushed out one of the girls, and took the girl's position. She danced spiritedly for about five minutes and then returned among the spectators. The onlookers roared with laughter at this performance, but the woman's expression was one of mock seriousness and anger. Another woman brandishing a rifle also ran to the dancers. She pointed the weapon at the feet of one of the girls and pretended to fire it.

One of the women of the household in which I lived explained that these women were the boy dancers' *kiyû·* and that they were "publicly displaying their jealousy and anger for their *ʔèˑsèŋ*'s girl partners."

When a brother's son marries, his *kiyû·*, with other women of her clan, protests the marriage by attacking the boy's mother and the mother's sisters.[31] Even after a brother's son is married, his *kiyû·* visits him and teases his wife, "pretending to make love to him."

A *kiyû·* is "proud" of her *ʔèˑsèŋ*'s participation in social and ceremonial dances and helps prepare food for him. In return, an *ʔèˑsèŋ* performs various services for his *kiyû·*. He may make furniture or repair household fixtures for her. One of the sons of my hosts, for example, made and installed window screens for his *kiyû·*. Formerly an *ʔèˑsèŋ* brought his *kiyû·* meat from game that he had killed and salt from salt expeditions. Mutually the relationship is informal, affectionate, and lifelong. In the presence of each other's spouses the two "pretend to be like lovers" and speak of their deep attachment for one another, "to make the husband or wife jealous."

Father's Sister ⟵⟶ Brother's Daughter

kiyû· ⟵――――――――⟶ *ʔèˑkʷíyoh*

kiyû· participates in the naming ceremony of her *ʔèˑkʷíyoh* and protects, aids, and provides affection at crucial periods in the girl's development. She guides her *ʔèˑkʷíyoh* through the puberty ceremonies at the time of the girl's first menstruation. As adults, the two visit one another frequently, confide in each other, and assist in household duties.

Maternal Grandmother ⟵⟶ Grandchild

sayâ· ⟵――――――――⟶ *sayâ·ʔèˑ*

Mother's mother and mother's mother's sister are called *sayâ·*; the reciprocal is *sayâ·ʔèˑ*, grandmother (diminutive). The behavior of *sayâ·* toward her *sayâ·ʔèˑ* is more indulgent and kind than that of a mother toward her child. Since a grandmother ordinarily lives in the same household as her grandchildren, she has frequent contacts with them. She rarely scolds a grandchild but provides a great deal of affection. A grandmother tells her grandchild stories and legends and instills in the

―――――――――

[30] See section on "Social Control," below.
[31] See section on "Life Cycle," below.

young Hopi-Tewa child a pride in being Hopi-Tewa. A *sayâ·* is loved dearly. A child will often seek her out in order to divulge his troubles to her, and he is always assured of a sympathetic reception and kindly counsel. While *sayâ·* is strong and active, she is the head of the household and in charge of all foodstuffs. She possesses essential ritual knowledge and must be consulted in all important matters regarding the household and clan.

The *sayâ·* of the household in which I lived fully met these requirements and performed her duties as a good grandmother. Her grandchildren respected, obeyed, and loved her. They sought her out to confide in her and to have her arbitrate quarrels between themselves and others. One of the girls slept with her every night on a sheepskin pallet. The two youngest children in the household, a boy of two and a girl of four, always took a position beside their grandmother when visitors came. If they were teased, they hid behind her or buried their faces in her lap while *sayâ·* spoke softly to them and stroked their hair.

The Hopi-Tewa recognize two relatives above the grandparent generation: *pahpá·*, mother's mother's mother, and her brother, *pép?ê·*. These relatives are usually extremely old and often are blind. Inevitably, then, the duty of their great-grandchildren and great-grandnephews and -nieces is to see that they are conducted about the village and guided into the houses of their relatives. A *pahpá·* or *pép'ê·* is kindly and indulgent to all and is respected and treated with respect by all members of the community.

Maternal and Paternal Grandfather ⟵⟶ Grandchild

θeté· ⟵————————————⟶ *θeté·?è·*

θeté·, grandfather, is applied to a grandfather, either maternal or paternal, and also to his brothers. Behavior of *θeté·* toward his grandchildren is marked by kindness and deep affection. If a grandfather is still strong and vigorous he may take his grandchild or grandnephew with him when he goes into the fields and there teach him the simple farming techniques of the Hopi and Hopi-Tewa. He will also guide him in other tasks, patiently and affectionately watching to see that the boy does a good job. If the grandfather is Hopi-Tewa, he will tell his grandchild all about the Hopi-Tewa migration legend and the curse on the Hopi, and he will teach him Hopi-Tewa songs. Very old Hopi-Tewa are extremely proud of their Tewa heritage and try under all circumstances to develop such pride in younger children.

A middle-aged, acculturated Hopi-Tewa man gave me the following account of his boyhood relations with his maternal grandfather:

Whenever I went to see *θeté·* he made me sit beside him and told me the Hopi-Tewa migration legend which I had heard countless times from his lips.[32] I knew the story so well that I could probably relate it better than he. *θeté·* would start from the beginning, repeating all important events four times, as is the traditional pattern in all legends. His voice would become charged with emotion when he spoke of the injustices the Hopi-Tewa suffered from the Hopi, and he always ended the legend by telling me that we Hopi-Tewa must never forget this story, but must always tell it to our children as he had related it to me. I became so tired of the story that I would try to invent some excuse so that I would not have to listen to it again. Sometimes I went to sleep while he was telling the story, and then he would shake me gently and tell me that I must not sleep, that the story was very important, and that I must learn it well. Sometimes I became angry with

[32] See "Hopi-Tewa and Hopi Relations," in chap. ii, and "Land," in chap. v, for partial accounts of the Hopi-Tewa migration legend.

θeté·; surely the Hopi were not as bad as he would have me believe. My own father is Hopi and I love my father dearly and all of my *kiyû·* are wonderful to me. But my grandfather was old and I did not want to offend him by telling him these things or by going away without hearing the end of the story.

The term *θeté·* is also used for father's sister's husband; actually, any man married to a woman of father's clan is called *θeté·*. A joking relationship exists between these relatives and ego. They constantly belittle one another. They invent uncomplimentary nicknames for each other and use them at social gatherings to provide humorous entertainment for all present. On one occasion I happened upon a spirited wrestling match between two Hopi-Tewa I knew intimately. Ordinarily, Hopi and Hopi-Tewa do not fight; but these two actually seemed angry at one another, and they struggled earnestly for almost an hour. A group of onlookers gathered; from their laughter and comments I soon learned that these two men were *θeté·* and *θeté·ʔè·*

Relations between a woman and her father's clanwomen's husbands also involve joking and name-calling, but no physical contacts occur between them.

Paternal Grandmother ⟵⟶ Grandchild

kuk'û· ⟵————————⟶ *kuʔè·*

Paternal grandmother is called *kuk'û·* if she has cut the umbilical cord and conducted the naming ceremony. The reciprocal is *kuʔè·*, umbilical-cord cutter (diminutive). The relationship between *kuk'û·* and her grandchild is similar to that between *sayâ·* and the latter's grandchild. If *kuk'û·* is young, however, she may behave toward her grandchild very much as a *kiyû·* does to her *ʔè·sèŋ* and *ʔè·kʷíyoh. kuk'û·* will protect and aid her grandchild during the child's growth and development. More frequently, however, the relation between *kuk'û·* and her grandchild is kindly, indulgent, and affectionate.

Mother's father's sisters and father's father's sisters are called *θeté·kʷíyoh*, grandfather women. Contact with these relatives is infrequent, but the relations that exist are similar to those between *sayâ·* and her grandchildren. They are kind and affectionate.

In-laws: *yaʔâ·*

Clansman's wife: *saⁱ*

Clanswoman's husband: *soyìŋgih*

The parents and relatives of a spouse are called collectively *yaʔâ·*, in-laws. A wife's or husband's father is *yaséno*, relative man; a wife's or husband's mother is *yakʷíyoh*, relative woman.

Men marrying into the household and clan are called *soyìŋgih*, male relatives-in-law. They are regarded with respect and affection, and their contributions to the economic coöperative activities of the household are fully appreciated. (See husband-wife relationship, above.)

Women marrying into the household and clan are called *saⁱ*, female relatives-in-law. Despite the fact of matrilocal residence, married women often go with their husbands to visit the household of his birth, and they not infrequently aid their husband's relatives in the preparation of food and other duties at feast times. Members of a household are usually quite proud of their *saⁱ* and often boast about her beauty and accomplishments. Since I was considered a clan member in the household in which I had resided during the initial stages of my research, my wife became their *sa*ⁱ. On one occasion my wife made a special cake to be taken to *mɛmɛ́h* (my hostess's brother) in the kiva where he was in retreat, preparing for an important ceremony. Several days later when I saw some of the men who had also been in retreat, they remarked how much they had enjoyed the cake. "You should have heard your *mɛmɛ́h*," they said. "He boasted about your wife all evening. Not only was *sa*ⁱ a very beautiful girl but she was also a most wonderful cook!"

THE LIFE CYCLE

It is important to consider the life cycle before summarizing and noting the significant aspects of the kinship system. An account of the development of an individual from birth to death will clarify the relations and behavior between the various relatives already discussed and give us a better understanding of how a Hopi-Tewa becomes a participating member of his culture.

During the period of the study I became intimately acquainted with several Hopi-Tewa households. The individuals in these households range from the newly born to the very old. Several children were born when I was staying in Tewa Village. A number of the children were born in the hospital at Keams Canyon, and the customary ritual was not, of course, carried out completely. Even in such cases, however, the naming ceremony is performed for the child as soon as it is returned to the village. Hopi-Tewa women usually try to have their babies in the village in the traditional manner, but in recent years a few women have been persuaded by government employees and white friends to go to the hospital. I was not able to attend any of the native birth rites[33] but obtained the following brief account from the senior woman of the household in which I resided:

If my daughter is going to have a baby she will have it in this house. I will call my sister and also my sister's older daughters who have already had children. We will darken the room by hanging blankets over the door and windows. Only the women will be present, none of the men. If she has trouble having the child, we may call a "doctor" [a native medicine man] to help her. After the child is born I will call my *yakᵂⁱyoh*, my daughter's husband's mother, and she will cut the umbilical cord. *yakᵂⁱyoh* [called *kù·kuh* by the child after it is grown] cuts the cord with an arrow shaft if the baby is a boy and with a corn-gruel stirring rod if the baby is a girl. She then places fine ashes on the navel.

After the baby is born my daughter and her baby are cared for by her *yakᵂⁱyoh* [women of her husband's clan] for twenty days. They comb and bathe my daughter and make certain that she is kept warm all of the time. She is given hot *ʔqkὲŋ* [corn-meal gruel] and may drink only boiled juniper water; she cannot have pure water, meat, or salt. The baby is washed right after birth by *yakᵂⁱyoh* and sprinkled with fine ashes. This is repeated every four days for the twenty days that my daughter and her baby are in confinement in the darkened house. An ear of white corn is kept next to the baby all of the time "to guard the baby."

On the nineteenth day the women of my house and my sisters' houses [women of the extended household] prepare piki, corn pudding, stews, and other food. Before sunrise the next day all the women of my daughter's husband's clan come to the house. Each woman dips an ear of corn in a bowl of yucca suds and touches the head of the baby four times and then with a prayer gives it a name. The name is from her clan—something which describes her clan. If the baby's father is Tobacco clan, the baby may be named *sahpovi*, tobacco blossom; or maybe *kà·c'é·*, yellow leaf, describing the tobacco plant when it is ripe. As the sun comes up, *yakᵂⁱyoh* takes the baby outside and utters all the names that have been given to it. Out of the many names, the baby's mother and father will decide which is the prettiest and will call the baby by that name."

[33] Parsons (1921a, pp. 98–104) gives a First Mesa Hopi account of birth rites with certain references to Hopi-Tewa practices.

The infant is nursed by the mother and is cared for primarily by her, but almost immediately he begins to become a real part of the extended household: his brothers and sisters and his mother's sisters and their children start playing an important role in his training soon after his birth. *sayâ·*, mother's mother, is also frequently on the scene. For the first six or seven years of life, socialization takes place almost entirely within the confines of the extended household. At the age of six or seven, however, the child starts to school at the day school. This takes him out of the secure and familiar surroundings of the household for the first time.

The day school can be either a relatively easy adjustment for the child or a seriously disturbing one. Under a patient and indulgent teacher the transition may even be a pleasant one, opening new experiences and new horizons for the child. Unfortunately, such teachers are in the minority. Although a teacher may sincerely wish to adjust Hopi and Hopi-Tewa children comfortably into an unfamiliar situation, the teacher's own value orientation is often completely different. The ordinary American teacher on an Indian reservation tries to instill in his pupils such American principles as saving, individual responsibility, competition, and a dozen others entirely alien to the Hopi or Hopi-Tewa child. In the process, the child becomes considerably confused, and disturbance to the child's personality structure may result. Not only do the goals of his teachers conflict with those of a child's traditional cultural values and training, but the child is suddenly confronted with a puzzling and bewildering maze of new technological equipment to which he must adjust: washbasins, toilets, pencils, papers, and a myriad other new things not present in his home environment.

Hopi-Tewa children are perhaps more fortunate in the school situation than Hopi children. The more aggressive characteristics of the Hopi-Tewa generally and the fact that they are or have been in the recent past a minority group (with respect to the Hopi) have made them more receptive to American cultural values. Moreover, the necessity of having to learn a new language is not a strange phenomenon to a Hopi-Tewa child. Hopi-Tewa children have been in a bilingual situation for more than 250 years. A child learns Shoshonean Hopi almost simultaneously with Tewa. English is not an entirely unfamiliar language either. He has heard his parents, his brothers, and his sisters use it on various occasions. I have many times, for instance, observed adult Hopi-Tewa teaching young relatives English words and delighting in the successful attempts of the children in mastering a few words.

When not in school a boy accompanies his father to the fields and slowly learns about farming through observation and by actually doing some of the work. A girl also learns household duties in the same way, from the women of the household.

Between eight and ten years of age, both boys and girls are initiated into the katcina cult. A ceremonial father is selected for the boy and a ceremonial mother for the girl. These sponsors are from a clan other than that of the child. The initiation rites are held four days before Powamu—a Hopi ceremony in which the Hopi-Tewa participate. Parents, ceremonial sponsors, and all the acquaintances of a child have dramatized and made these activities extremely important in his thinking. A child who is going to be initiated exhibits tremendous excitement long before the event takes place. A Hopi-Tewa said:

We were told that the katcina were beings from another world. There were some boys who said that they were not, but we could never be sure, and most of us believed what we were told. Our own parents and elders tried to make us believe that the katcina were powerful beings, some good and some bad, and that they knew our innermost thoughts and actions. If they did not know about us through their own great power, then probably our own relatives told the katcina about us. At any rate every time they visited us they seemed to know what we had thought and how we had acted.

As the time for our initiation came closer we became more and more frightened. The ogre katcina, the Soyoku, came every year and threatened to carry us away; now we were told that we were going to face these awful creatures. Though we were told not to be afraid, we could not help ourselves. If the katcina are really supernatural and powerful beings, we might have offended them by some thought or act and they might punish us. They might even take us with them as the Soyoku threatened to do every year.

Four days before Powamu our ceremonial fathers and our ceremonial mothers took us to the Central Plaza Kiva. The girls were accompanied by their ceremonial mothers, and we boys by our ceremonial fathers. We stood outside the kiva, and then two whipper katcina, looking very mean, came out of the kiva. Only a blanket covered the nakedness of the boys, and as the katcina drew near our ceremonial fathers removed the blanket. The girls were permitted to keep on their dresses, however. Our ceremonial parents urged us to offer sacred corn meal to the katcina; as soon as we did so they whipped us with their yucca whips. I was hit so hard that I defecated and urinated and I could feel the welts forming on my back and I knew that I was bleeding too. He whipped me four times, but the last time he hit me on the leg instead, and as the whipper started to strike again, my ceremonial father pulled me back and he took the blow himself. "This is a good boy, my old man," he said to the katcina. "You have hit him enough."

For many days my back hurt and I had to sleep on my side until the wounds healed.

After the whipping a small sacred feather was tied to our hair and we were told not to eat meat or salt. Four days later we went to see the Powamu ceremony in the kiva. As babies, our mother had taken us to see this event; but as soon as we began to talk, they stopped taking us. I could not remember what had happened on Powamu night and I was afraid that another frightening ordeal awaited us. Those of us who were whipped went with our ceremonial parents. In this dance we saw that the katcina were our own fathers, uncles, and brothers. This made me feel strange. I felt somehow that all my relatives were responsible for the whipping we had received. My ceremonial father was kind and gentle during this time and I felt very warm toward him, but I also wondered if he was to blame for our treatment. I felt deceived and ill-treated.

After the Powamu ceremony my head was washed and I received a new name. At this time, too, the small feather was removed from my hair and the food restrictions were lifted.

The traumatic experiences of the katcina initiation are deeply embedded in the memory of all my informants. Yet most of them felt that the whippings were not harmful but on the contrary were good for the child. Although no relative will lay a hand on a child, the whippings of the katcina are considered to have a favorable effect on the subsequent behavior of the individual. There were similar expressions of opinion among those with whom I talked about the subject. "Hopi and Hopi-Tewa children are well-behaved because they are disciplined early in life." "A human being needs to be broken, like a horse, before he can become a well-behaved individual." Many of the older Hopi-Tewa ascribe the "meanness" of school-trained boys and girls to the fact that they have not gone through this experience. For the same reason some parents defend the old military type of government boarding school where children were heavily disciplined. Missionary boarding schools, which follow a rather strict regime, are also preferred by some to the more informal and relaxed modern government boarding schools.

After initiation, Hopi-Tewa children begin to take a more active part in household duties, farming, and ranching activities. They are also qualified to impersonate katcina characters after the first initiation and soon assume such roles. Schooling provided by the day school ends about the time a boy or a girl has reached the age of fourteen or fifteen. At this time another important event awaits them. For the boy the event is membership in the Hopi-Tewa Winter Solstice Society, and the initiation is generally simple but of great significance. After this event a boy is considered a man and is eligible for active membership in other Hopi-Tewa religious societies. A few Hopi-Tewa men also join the tribal societies of the Hopi after gaining membership in the Hopi-Tewa Winter Solstice Society (see chap. iv, n. 30).

A ceremonial father, generally not the same as the previous one, is selected for the boy.[34] The ceremonial father must be a man who is not of the boy's clan, but a man whose clan belongs to the same kiva group with which the boy's clan is affiliated.[35]

Four days before the Winter Solstice ceremony, in December, the boy abstains from meat and salt. He is constantly in the care of his ceremonial father; he eats his meals at the man's home and also sleeps there. Finally on the night of the fourth day he accompanies his ceremonial father to the kiva. If his clan is affiliated with the Central Plaza Kiva he goes into that one; if he belongs to the Outside Kiva, he enters that one. The Winter Solstice ceremony is an all-night affair. To members the event is announced sixteen days before, and prayer sticks are made by the members who are in retreat there. The final night of the ceremony consists of the singing of songs and the telling of migration legends and Hopi-Tewa experiences by the chief of the group of clans that belong to that kiva. The novitiates sit next to their ceremonial fathers and listen attentively in order to learn the songs, legends, and stories told that night. The retreat terminates just before daybreak when the manufactured prayer sticks are taken out and deposited in the various shrines and springs in the Hopi-Tewa area. The ceremony is strictly a Hopi-Tewa one; no Hopi are permitted to attend.

The second important event in a girl's life occurs at the time of her first menstruation. A woman keeps close watch over her daughter and instructs her to report all her physiological symptoms. When a mother is informed by her daughter that her menstrual period has begun, she brings one of her husband's sisters, the girl's *kiyû·*. This woman then takes charge of the girl. She is secluded in the grinding room of *kiyû·*'s house and grinds corn for four days. During this time she abstains from meat and salt and must use a scratching stick to scratch herself. In her chores she is assisted by her *kiyû·*, one of whom is constantly with her. There is a general atmosphere of good-natured humor, and the conversation is informal and lively. At the end of the four days, one of the *kiyû·* washes the novitiate's hair and fixes it in the "cart wheel" fashion of the Hopi. The girl is also given a new name at this time.

The foregoing sketch of a girl's puberty rite was given as a definite "ideal." My informants admitted that this custom was no longer consistently observed. My hostess told me that only a very few Hopi-Tewa girls go through this ceremony at the present time. Her own daughter had at first objected to doing so, but had been persuaded to observe the ritual. The first initiation—the katcina initiation—is in fact observed religiously, according to my hostess. She remarked:

> We still have control of our children when they are young, but schools and white contacts make them so independent that by the time they are twelve or fourteen they are difficult to manage.

[34] The ceremonial father for katcina initiation may be a Hopi, but for entrance into the Winter Solstice Society, the sponsor must be a Hopi-Tewa man. Therefore a boy's sponsors for katcina and the Winter Solstice Society often are two different persons.

[35] For a discussion of clans and kiva groups, see chap. iv.

They get mad when we tell them to go through the rites. Schoolgirls generally hate to grind corn, and we old women have to do it all the time. The boys are better—they do not mind going to the kiva and performing their duties like their uncles and ceremonial fathers tell them to do.

Indeed, the Winter Solstice Society has no trouble drawing new members. This is probably because the initiation rites are not difficult and involved, but on the contrary are even pleasurable. The twenty-six-year-old youth in the household in which I resided told me that "it was fun to attend the Winter Solstice ceremony and listen to the old Hopi-Tewa songs and to hear the old men tell of the experiences of our forefathers."

After a boy's initiation into the Winter Solstice Society and a girl's participation in the puberty ceremony, they are theoretically ready for marriage. Hopi-Tewa marriages, however, do not ordinarily take place until a youth is between twenty and twenty-five and a girl between eighteen and twenty-two. Courtship is, like that of the Hopi, strictly in the hands of the two persons concerned (see Eggan, 1950, p. 54). Marriage restrictions are based on kinship[36] and, except for the one prohibiting marriage within one's own clan, are not generally observed at present. Marriage between a couple belonging to the same clan is strictly prohibited, however, and there was not a single violation of this rule in the marriages recorded at the time of this study. Although marriage is an individual matter, opinions of a person's siblings and father's sisters have an important influence on his choice of a mate.

Boys and girls have a maximum opportunity to see each other. Parents or other members of the household do not keep a check on the activities of their grown children. Boys and girls meet under the protecting eaves of the cliffs, around the trading post, or in the proximity of the day school during the evenings. Although, according to reports, formerly a boy stole in late at night to where a girl slept in her house, this is no longer a customary pattern of courtship. Premarital sexual relations are the rule, and the birth of children before marriage is common. Generally, however, a girl marries the father of her child and tries to do so before her child is born.

Marriage customs are similar to those of the Hopi as reported in the existing literature.[37] Marriages usually take place in January and August. According to Hopi-Tewa belief, marriages should not be contracted in the katcina season, from February through July. January and August are considered the months for gaiety, the time when social dances and other happy events take place.

When a couple has decided to marry, the girl presents the boy's mother with piki and receives meat in exchange. Then follows a period of several weeks in which the women of the girl's household grind corn. When a large amount of corn has been ground, the girl is dressed in traditional Hopi-Tewa dress and her hair is fixed in "cart wheels." The girl is then taken to the house of the boy by her maternal and paternal kinswomen. The girl grinds corn in the boy's house for three days, and early on the fourth morning her hair is washed by the boy's maternal kinswomen.

While the girl is in her prospective husband's household, the boy's father's clans-

---

[36] See above, p. 311.
[37] See Titiev, 1944, pp. 30–43, and Eggan, 1950, pp. 53–57. Parsons (1921*b*, pp. 259–265) records two versions of a marriage account by a Hopi-Tewa man and woman. These accounts closely parallel the description I obtained.

women may "object" to the marriage. These women descend on the boy's house and bedaub his mother and sisters with mud for letting their ʔè·sèŋ get away from them. They speak slightingly of the bride, saying that she does not deserve so fine a husband, and point out her flaws in personality and appearance. This is all done, however, in a spirit of fun, and any damage is later paid for.

In the meantime, the boy's male relatives on both his father's and his mother's side prepare the girl's wedding garments—these consist of belt, robe, dress, and moccasins. When the garments are completed, the girl dons the new outfit and her hair is dressed in the style of Hopi-Tewa married women.[38] She and her husband are then taken by his mother to her (the mother's) house. Early the next morning the boy's head is washed by the girl's clanswomen. The corn meal ground in the preceding weeks by the girl's relatives is then taken to the boy's household "as payment for depriving the family of a worker."

In addition to ground meal, enormous amounts of other food are taken to the boy's house. In this practice, Tewa Village appears to differ from the Hopi generally. A Hopi teacher at Shongopovi told me that none of the Hopi villages matched the Hopi-Tewa community in the amounts of food brought. Indeed, there is an effort on the part of the girl's relatives to bring more food and to display it more elaborately in front of the bridegroom's mother's home than was done for any previous marriage. In this respect there is a real spirit of competition.

Marriages in the traditional manner, as described above, are still popular. Couples who are married in a church or by a justice of the peace will return to have an "Indian wedding" as soon as possible. Sometimes the traditional wedding is performed first, and then the couple goes through a civil or church ceremony.

Residence is matrilocal, despite the fact that a couple may live separately in a part of the girl's mother's house or may even build a new home in another part of the village or at Polacca. The term "matrilocal residence" is justified because the new residence is built primarily with the help of the girl's extended family and on her clan lands. After the couple has started housekeeping, interaction is primarily with the wife's relatives, as illustrated in the discussion of the household printed above.

As time passes, a man becomes more and more entrenched in his new household. He forms ties that bind him ever more strongly to the relatives of his wife. The longer the two remain together, the more secure the marriage tie becomes. We have already seen that children are the main factor in keeping a couple together; perhaps equally as important are the well-working relationships a man establishes with his wife's relatives.

The Hopi-Tewa believe that sickness is caused by bad thoughts, quarreling, witchcraft, and the breech of taboo. Hopi-Tewa ceremonialism and the admonitions of the Village Chief, Outside Chief, clan chiefs, society chiefs, and maternal uncles constantly emphasize the necessity of purging oneself and the community of these disease-producing agents.[39] Prayer sticks and prayer feathers made by members of a ceremonial society during its retreat or by a group preparing to put on a "social

[38] This hair style differs from that of the Hopi; it is similar to that of the Rio Grande Tewa in that the sides are clipped. Hopi married women part the hair and with a string twist the locks on either side of the face.

[39] The ceremonial aspects of Hopi-Tewa life mentioned here in relation to sickness are discussed in greater detail in chap. iv.

dance," are placed in the shrines in order to induce the gods to keep the community healthy and the environment appeased.[40] Social dances and repeat performances of katcina dances are requested by individuals for advancing personal, family, and community well-being. Public appearances of social dancers, ceremonial society members, and katcina performers are "made beautiful and exacting" in order to impress the supernaturals and thus ensure for the people the blessings of good health and a bountiful harvest. The people must "have good thoughts and not be angry at anyone, nor quarrel with one another." This is important at all times, but it is vital during important ceremonials: "Some people are witches and they are trying to cause illness and the failure of crops; it is therefore important to counteract these evil influences by concentrating on the proper performances of ceremonials." Ceremonial leaders warn initiates and participants in the various ceremonies to observe the exacting ritual carefully and to guard against the breaking of food restrictions and sexual-continence regulations. The Hopi-Tewa believe that only by strict observance of all these rules can the community be assured of a healthy existence.

The Hopi-Tewa thus attempt to appease the environment and ward off illness by ceremonial activity and through the constant vigilance and admonitions of ceremonial leaders. In addition—on an individual level—a person who has a serious ailment may be dedicated to a "doctor father" or may engage the services of a medicine man.[41] An individual may also help cure an illness or injury by sprinkling sacred meal on the katcina dancers in a kiva or plaza performance. Another method, believed to be similarly efficacious, is to submit voluntarily to a whipping by the Whipper Katcina during the katcina initiation rites in February.

Failure of the community to observe the above precautions, or to prevent sickness by prescribed methods, results in drought, disease, and death. Death in old age is considered natural, but death in the prime of life is always attributed to one of the disease-producing agents discussed above. The Hopi-Tewa are reluctant to discuss death practices, and I was able to obtain only the barest information. No formal or ceremonial wailing is practiced; the body is interred as quickly as possible. A woman is buried in her wedding outfit; a man is wrapped in a blanket. Burial grounds are at the foot of the mesa on the southeast side. After burial, the relatives of the deceased avoid mentioning his name and refrain from commenting about the circumstances surrounding his death.

SUMMARY

From the above discussion of the kinship system and the life cycle, we see that the Hopi-Tewa emphasize the matrilineal household and lineage. The primary relationships involving authority and control are centered in the matrilineal, matrilocal household. The women of ego's lineage have the duty and responsibility of running the household; the mother's brother is charged with primary disciplinary powers. The father and his sisters and brothers, on the other hand, have a very different relationship to ego. Except for the father, these kin live in a different household. They have no authority in managing ego's household or in disciplining him: their relationship to ego is one of mutual aid and affection.

A third set of relatives provides an interesting function in the socialization of the

---

[40] That is, to prevent inclement weather and to provide abundant moisture for crops.

[41] Injuries and the common communicable diseases are now referred to the agency doctor, but lingering illnesses such as rheumatism and similar maladies are treated by medicine men.

individual. These are the husbands of father's sisters, who may joke and even engage in physical fights with male ego. He is permitted to retaliate and does so with increasing vigor and frequency as he gets older. A girl or woman may also engage in loud talk, "pretending to be angry" with her father's sister's husbands, but does not strike them.

Thus we see that along with the emphasis of the matrilineal household and lineage the Hopi-Tewa kinship system also channelizes behavior in an interesting manner among three sets of relatives. Authority and control is the prerogative of ego's mother and her sisters and brothers; affection is afforded primarily by the father and his brothers and sisters; whereas the release of aggression is provided by the father's sisters' husbands.[42]

The differences in the kinship system of the Hopi and that of the Hopi-Tewa are worth repeating. Along with the retention of their Tewa language, the Hopi-Tewa have also retained kinship terms that are the same or obviously cognate with Rio Grande Tewa terms. In behavior, the Hopi-Tewa husband-wife bond is more enduring than among the Hopi. Whereas the Hopi make little distinction between father and his brothers and between mother and her sisters, the Hopi-Tewa draw sharp distinctions between these relatives. Among the Hopi-Tewa, the mother's sisters are differentiated terminologically as older and younger, and differential treatment is accorded them—a distinction not made by the Hopi. Similarly, older siblings are accorded greater respect and obedience by the Hopi-Tewa. These differences in behavior appear to be vestigial holdovers from the bilateral, generational kinship system of the Rio Grande Tewa.

Changes in the kinship system as a result of modern conditions are evident primarily in the extended household. Interaction brought about by wage work and livestock activities is breaking up the household unit and dispersing its members in terms of nuclear family groups. However, since social and ceremonial functions bring about frequent resumptions of extended-household living, the integrity of the household unit still has great significance to the Hopi-Tewa. The deep satisfactions derived from social interaction and ceremonies are important in this respect, and so too is the automobile, which makes it possible for members of the extended household to interact frequently.

Analysis of the life cycle has also revealed another area in which modern pressures have brought about changes. Hopi-Tewa girls are resisting traditional patterns of work, particularly those connected with puberty rites. Girls are bobbing their hair and are objecting to the tedious roles of grinding corn. The number of girls who go through the puberty ceremonies is admittedly decreasing. Changes in the roles of men with respect to the life cycle are not pronounced. We shall see, however, that there are marked changes in the ceremonial system—an area of Hopi-Tewa culture in which men have a prominent role. The other significant events in a person's life— birth, marriage, and death practices—appear to be less affected by modern pressures.

Thus, despite changes and increasing pressures from the outside world, the Hopi-Tewa kinship system is still remarkably strong and functional at the present time.

---

[42] For women the customs prevalent at the time of marriage, when the bridegroom's father's clanswomen descend on his house and vigorously protest the marriage, provide another social release of aggression.

THE CLAN

The Hopi-Tewa clan resembles the Hopi clan in all its structural features. Certain basic Hopi concepts—particularly those concerned with phratral groupings and separate clan migration legends—appear to be new to the Hopi-Tewa. In recent years, however, there is clearly an indication that the Hopi-Tewa are attempting to adapt and adjust their own clan concepts to correspond with those of the Hopi. These efforts of the Hopi-Tewa to accommodate to Hopi clan concepts disclose subtle but important factors in the trend toward acculturation noted in chapter ii and discussed in greater detail in this and the following chapters.

Characteristics of Hopi-Tewa clan organization are revealed in the following statement by a Bear clansman:

> *kè·t'owah ʔò mù·*. I am of the Bear clan. Our *pahpâ·ʔìŋ* mothers' mothers' mothers and our *pép'ê·ʔìŋ*, mothers' mothers' mothers' brothers, were *kè·t'owah*, Bear clan people. They came a long, long, time ago from *c'ęwadéh*, our home in the east. Our *pép'ê·ʔê·*, sisters' daughters' daughters' children, as long as women of my clan have children, will be of the Bear clan. These are our *matuìŋ*, clan relatives, whom we trust, work with, and confide in. *kayê·*, my mother's older sister, guards the sacred fetish *kɨ·luhʔà·*, which is the power and guardian of our clan and which was brought in the migration from *c'ęwadéh*. *káyê·* feeds our *kɨ·luhʔà·* and sees that the feathers are always properly dressed. At important ceremonies, *mɛmêh*, my mother's brother, erects his altar and sets our *kɨ·luh'à·* in a prominent place within the altar. *káyê· and mɛmêh* make all the important decisions for our clan, and such decisions are accepted with respect and obedience by all Bear clan members. *káyê·* and *mɛmêh* are called upon to advise, to reprimand, and to make decisions on land and ritual affairs for all of us who are of the Bear clan. *káyê·*'s house is where our *kɨ·luhʔà·* is kept, and therefore it is a sacred house to us and there we go for all important matters that concern our clan.

To complete the foregoing description, a few additional remarks about the nature of the Hopi-Tewa clan are necessary. Marriage between members of the same clan is strictly prohibited, and no violation of this rule appears in the record of Hopi-Tewa marriages. Clans are landholding units, each clan having certain lands set aside for the use of its members. The control of ceremonies and their ritual paraphernalia are in the keeping of certain clans. Adopted children retain the clan of their mothers —in all cases of adoption at Tewa Village, however, the children were adopted by members of their own clan. Kinship terms and behavior patterns present in the lineage are extended to embrace all members of the clan.

The similarities between Hopi-Tewa clans and Hopi clans (cf. Eggan, 1950, p. 62) may be accounted for in any of the following ways: (1) the clans brought over may have been like those of the Hopi at that time; (2) "clan names" similar to those of the present Rio Grande Tewa may have been reinterpreted and reorganized into the clans of the Hopi type soon after the Tewa arrived at Hopi; or (3) the present Hopi-Tewa system may have been borrowed very early from the Hopi.

Of the three possibilities, the second one seems the most likely. As we have seen in the historical section, the Tanoan-speaking peoples probably did not have clans when they moved into the upper Rio Grande area. They were exposed quite early to "Western" influences, however, by a migration of a new people—possibly the Keres—into the area.[43] This migrant group is believed to have been characterized by the following traits: clans, masks, the katcina cult, medicine societies, female

---

[43] See section on "Early History and Culture," in chap. i.

descent, and female house ownership. Some of these traits are now present in attenuated form among the Rio Grande Tanoan pueblos.

The Rio Grande Tewa today group themselves in terms of "clan names."[44] We cannot equate these "clan names" with clans, however, because the groups so called have neither function nor clearly defined patterns of descent and residence.[45] These "clans" have nothing to do with ceremonial or economic affairs, land or house control, political organization, or the regulation of marriage. Informants among the Rio Grande Tewa state variously that one acquires such a "clan" from the father or the mother (Hill MS). It appears then that, among the Rio Grande Tewa at least, the borrowing of the clan from the diffusing agents—possibly the Keres—was arrested before it became a significant part of their social organization. Possibly, Spanish influences acted as a deterrent to the diffusion of clan concepts, particularly since the Spanish colonists were strongly patrilineal. At any rate, only "clan names" exist among the Rio Grande Tewa at present, and it is very probable that the migrant Tano group at Hopi had a similar undeveloped clan organization. The idea of the clan was not foreign, however, and it is possible that this nuclear idea was developed quite early into an organization which approximated the Hopi clan. An early adaptation of the kinship and clan organizations would have facilitated the preservation of a distinctive way of life, which, as the present study indicates, the ancestors of the Hopi-Tewa desired. Hopi kinship and clan organizations stress matrilineal descent and matrilocal residence; thus, a Tewa mother, predisposed to emphasize the merits of her own culture, could do so effectively in the convenient atmosphere of her own pueblo and Tewa kin.

Rio Grande Tewa visitors are fully conscious of the importance of the clan among the Hopi and Hopi-Tewa. They have learned from experience, for instance, that they receive more cordial treatment in the homes of Hopi-Tewa whose clan corresponds to their "name clan" than they do from others; therefore they proudly announce their "clan" as soon as they arrive at Hopi. The following clans of the Hopi-Tewa[46] were found represented by Hodge (1896, pp. 345–352) among the "clan names" of the Rio Grande Tewa pueblos in 1896: Nambe—Bear, Tobacco, Cloud, and Earth; San Ildefonso—Cloud, Cottonwood, Fir (Wood), and Corn (several varieties); San Juan—Bear, Cloud, Earth, Fir (Wood), and Corn; Santa Clara—Cloud, Earth, Fir (Wood), Corn, and Cottonwood; Tesuque—Cloud. Each of these Rio Grande pueblos has other "clans" that are not represented at Tewa Village. Hopi-Tewa informants recognize these names and report that these clans were once present in Tewa Village but are now extinct.

A Hopi-Tewa asks a visitor from the Rio Grande Tewa pueblos, *"Hę· t'owah ?um mù·,* What clan are you?" When identity is established, the visitor is supposed to stay with his clan relatives, but he is welcome in any home at Tewa Village. If a man visitor comes to the village, everyone calls him *męmę́h,* mother's brother; if the visitor is a woman, *káyê·,* mother's older sister. These are terms ordinarily restricted to clan members; but out of respect, Tewa visitors are addressed in the same way as clan members. If a Rio Grande Tewa gives the name of a clan not represented at Tewa Village, the answer invariably is *"hodi ką́h,* they have become extinct." Any

---

[44] Hodge (1896, pp. 345–352) obtained a list of clan names among the Rio Grande Tewa.
[45] For basic requirements for a clan, see Murdock, 1949, pp. 68–69.
[46] See below, p. 335, and fig. 1, for a list of Hopi-Tewa clans.

Hopi-Tewa household will then take him in and treat him with kindness and respect—just as they would act toward a real member of the household and clan.

The Hopi-Tewa clan has apparently mirrored the Hopi clan in structure and function for a long time. Certain basic Hopi concepts, however, appear to be new to the Hopi-Tewa. One of these concepts has to do with clan linkage or phratry organization. Among the Hopi, all the clans are grouped into larger aggregates or phratries of two or more clans each. Eggan (1950, table 2, pp. 65–66) gives a list of some fifty clans grouped in twelve phratries for all the Hopi villages.[47] The phratry system appears to be an old and well-established practice among the Hopi. Eggan (1950, pp. 78–79) reports:

> The basic phratry pattern is more clearly delimited for the Hopi than are the constituent clan patterns. . . . It is evident that the phratry grouping has exerted an enormous stabilizing influence in Hopi society. Individual clans are subject to extinction from failure of the line or lines of women. This can happen rather rapidly, as the data for the last three generations indicate, particularly where the average population per clan group is small. The Hopi villages have been in existence since before 1540, the Oraibi at least probably before 1200. With our present knowledge of the mechanisms for clan change, the basic pattern can only be due to the importance and conservatism of the phratry pattern, unless we are willing to assume that the clan-phratry pattern is recent among the Hopi. This is denied by the central importance of the clan and the uniqueness of the phratry pattern for the Hopi . . .

Although there are seven Hopi-Tewa clans—Bear, Fir, Corn, Tobacco, Earth, Cloud, and Cottonwood—only two, Bear and Fir, are grouped together. This linkage seems identical with the phratry groupings of the Hopi and fits Titiev's definition of the Hopi phratry (Titiev, 1944, p. 58): ". . . a nameless division of kindred made up of two or more clans which share certain privileges, mainly ceremonial, in common. The outstanding feature of the phratry is that it delimits the greatest extension of kinship terms based on a given relationship, and that it marks the largest exogamic unit recognized by the Hopi . . ."

All informants agree that this linkage occurred as recently as fifty or sixty years ago.[48] The reason for merging is familiar Hopi theorizing.[49] According to some informants, the two clans combined because in a migration legend the Fir clan is mentioned as a "pathmaker" for the Bear clan. Members of the clan assert that partnership in the past legitimatizes the linkage. Other informants report that the Fir clan was taken as a partner by the Bear clan when the Sun clan became extinct, about fifty years ago.[50] The Sun clan, along with Bear, Corn, and Tobacco clans, made up the membership of the Central Plaza Kiva. According to these informants, the extinction of the Sun clan disturbed the proper performance of certain ceremonies and another clan was needed to take its place.[51] The Fir clan was therefore

[47] Eggan states that this list does not pretend to be exhaustive, but that he has examined most of the relevant literature.

[48] That the linkage of Fir and Bear clans is of recent occurrence is substantiated by the fact that neither Stephen nor Fewkes reports phratry groupings at Tewa Village. Since the linkage occurred about the time of changed attitudes toward the Hopi (see above, pp. 294 ff.), it indicated a willingness on the part of the Hopi-Tewa to learn about Hopi culture.

[49] Titiev (1944, pp. 55–56) and Eggan (1950, pp. 80–89) have discussed the basis for phratral groupings as conceived by the Hopi.

[50] Stephen (1936, p. 1084) lists the Sun Clan as still functioning in 1893; Parsons in 1920, however, notes its extinction.

[51] See chap. iv for ceremonial functions in which these clans participate.

brought in to fill the vacancy.[52] Kinship terms are extended to both clans, and marriages between members of the two clans are forbidden.

Members of the Fir and Cottonwood clans also consider themselves related to one another because "Fir and Cottonwood clans are both 'wood' or 'timber' clans." This grouping appears to be based on a familiar Hopi concept that "like" objects or "like" aspects of nature "belong together." On the same basis the Hopi-Tewa Cottonwood clan is equated with the Hopi Katcina clan "because katcina dolls are made from cottonwood." There are no shared privileges, ceremonial or otherwise, between Fir, Cottonwood, or Hopi Katcina clans; nor are kinship terms and behavior extended; neither is marriage restricted. My own belief is that this grouping represents the initial stages of a phratral linkage which may eventually reach the full status of a Hopi phratry. Bear and Fir are the only Hopi-Tewa clans linked in the Hopi fashion at present, that is, by (1) the sharing of certain ceremonial privileges; (2) extension of kinship terms and, at least among some members, shared behavioral patterns;[53] and (3) restriction of marriage between members of the two clans.

In good Hopi manner, members of the Bear and Fir clans now claim relationship to a host of clans present among the Hopi and other tribes. They rationalize this relationship not only on the basis that "like objects" or "like" aspects of nature belong together, but on the following principle. Hopi clans are considered to be "partners" if they have shared mutual experiences during the mythical wanderings following the emergence. Thus, for example, Hopi Parrot and Crow clans are equated because of the following migration legend:

When the Parrot people stopped for the night they perched their guide, parrot, on the branch of a tree. On one occasion they built a fire underneath the branch of the tree where the parrot had been placed. They forgot about the bird until they were about to move again, and when they looked up on the branch, they saw there a bird that looked like a crow. Some of the people said: "It is a crow, and we will take the name Crow for our people and descendants." That is why some people are Parrot clan and some Crow clan, but they are one people for they traveled together and did everything as a group.[54]

On the basis of such theories the Hopi-Tewa Fir and Bear clan members claim relationship to members of the Hopi Bear, Bear's Eyeball, Bear's Bones, Carrying Strap, Spider, and Bluebird clans. In addition, they believe themselves related to strictly Hopi-Tewa "clans" which have developed, in name at least, independently of the Hopi: Mexican, Red Coral, Yellowwood, Aspen, Pine, Wood, and Stick.[55]

An incipient linkage between the Cottonwood and Fir clans has not been carried out as far as that between the Bear and the Fir. The other four Hopi-Tewa clans—Tobacco, Corn, Earth, and Cloud—are not associated with other clans. These clans are present among the Hopi, or at least are recognized as "alternate" names in phratry groupings. Among the Hopi, for example, Corn clan is associated with

---

[52] Here is evidence that clans do merge to assume the ceremonial duties of an extinct clan. This possibility was conjectured by Lowie (1929, p. 310); Parsons (1936, p. xxxiii); Titiev (1944, p. 55); and Eggan (1950, p. 77).

[53] Another indication that the Fir-Bear clan linkage is recent is the fact that behavioral patterns are not shared by all members of the two clans.

[54] Related by a Hopi informant from the village of Sichomovi on First Mesa.

[55] These are only alternate names for clans and do not have actual representation. They occur, however, as the names of actual clans among Navaho, Rio Grande Pueblo, and other tribes and are therefore convenient to use for associating such clans with Hopi-Tewa Bear and Fir clans.

Cloud, Fog, Snow, and Patki (Water House). When I asked if the Hopi-Tewa Corn clan was also similarly related, my informant, a Corn clan woman, replied that the Tewa were not Hopi and she could not believe that a Hopi clan, even though similar in name, could be related to a Tewa clan. With regard to the association of Fir and Bear clans with certain Hopi clans, she remarked that these people "were trying to deny their Tewa heritage and wanted to be like Hopi." Yet when this same woman was on a visit to Mishongnovi in the winter of 1951 she sought out Patki households. At that time she remarked: "These are our people; they treat us kindly when we visit them, and when they come to our village they stay in our houses."

The remarks of this woman indicate the ambivalent attitude toward the Hopi already noted in chapter ii. It is my belief that the four Hopi-Tewa clans which at present are still retaining their distinctiveness will soon find a reason for merging among themselves and with other Hopi clans, and will thus form phratries in the Hopi manner.[56]

Tewa Village has two kivas: *mú·nɛ tèh*, Central Plaza Kiva, and *p'ɛndi tèh*, Outside Kiva. The seven Hopi-Tewa clans are divided into these two kivas. The following are Central Plaza Kiva clans: Bear, Fir, Corn, and Tobacco. The Outside Kiva clans are Earth, Cottonwood, and Cloud. Before the Fir clan merged with the Bear clan its members belonged to the Outside Kiva; thus, while representatives of the Sun clan still lived (the Sun clan was aligned with the clans of Central Plaza Kiva), the two Hopi-Tewa kivas were evenly balanced, each having four clans. Today the Cloud clan is almost extinct, since it has only one old woman of about seventy-five and three men left in it.[57] The clan is nevertheless important, since it controls the Shumakoli, the only society at Tewa Village having the curing of illness as its sole objective.

The division of clans in terms of the two kivas suggests the Rio Grande Tewa moiety system. Indeed, some Hopi-Tewa informants have used the Rio Grande Tewa terms *xayé·* (Summer) and *kʷɛdèh* (Winter) to designate Central Plaza Kiva and Outside Kiva groups, respectively. It is possible, of course, that this usage has been borrowed in recent years from the frequent visits of the Rio Grande Tewa; however, there are other aspects of Hopi-Tewa social organization which seem to reveal a vestigial moiety organization. These aspects are most pronounced in ceremonial life and are therefore reserved for discussion in the chapter "Ceremonial Organization."

Hopi concepts of clan migrations and relative position of clans in terms of status are also beginning to influence the Hopi-Tewa. The migration legends of the Hopi follow a characteristic pattern (see Eggan, 1950, p. 79). After the various Hopi clans emerged from the underworld, they set out in various directions and ultimately arrived at one or another of the Hopi villages. When a clan arrived in a Hopi village it secured land from the clan or clans that had preceded it. The new-

---

[56] This prediction is made in view of the precedent already set by Bear and Fir clans and because the trend in other areas of Hopi and Hopi-Tewa culture seems to point toward social and cultural integration on First Mesa.

[57] About fifty years ago a Hopi-Tewa Cloud woman married a Shongopovi man and moved with her family to his village. Tewa Village denounced her for this violation of matrilocal residence. Shongopovi people say that the family moved out because the Hopi-Tewa people were "mean" to her. Although the Cloud clan is extinct at Tewa Village, the clan is represented at Shongopovi by several female members of the clan. These women speak no Tewa but proudly assert that they are Tewa and not Shongopovi Hopi.

comers were given the land in exchange for their performing a ceremony or providing protection from marauding enemies. The priority of arrival of clans at Hopi was thus very important in terms of prestige and status, because, among other things, it determined land rights. The late arrivals were as a consequence relegated to more exposed sites in the villages and given poorer farm land. In terms of status, these late arrivals occupied the lowest positions. Hopi logic is not consistent, however; it appears that certain clans, though arriving late, have elevated themselves to higher positions. Such changes appear to have taken place under certain fortuitous circumstances, perhaps with the rise of unusually capable leaders in a low-ranking clan or through the phratry pattern in which a late-arriving clan might be incorporated into a league with important clans. In terms of clan migrations and the priority of clans at Hopi, Eggan (1950, p. 79) reports:

> ... The early ethnologists, particularly Fewkes [1902] accepted these [migration] legends at their face value and attempted to reconstruct Hopi history in accordance with them. But it soon became apparent that the origin legends of the same clan from different villages showed major contradictions and that even within the same village the stories of associated clans did not always correspond. And later research has suggested that the *order* of arrival of clans at various villages parallels their present ceremonial precedence.

The Hopi-Tewa clans have developed migration legends similar to the Hopi but with certain important differences. These clans believe that the migration of the Hopi-Tewa to Hopi took place in two groups—the clans of the Central Plaza Kiva coming first and those of the Outside Kiva following later.[58] This pattern differs from that of the Hopi, who conceive of the individual clans as coming to Hopi separately.

In terms of status, the Central Plaza Kiva clans claim that since they were the first to arrive on First Mesa, their position at Tewa Village is similar to that of the original Snake and Bear clans at Walpi.[59] Their role, they assert, is sacred; they must pray and meditate for the welfare of all Hopi-Tewa individuals. Among the Hopi, those clans believed to have arrived first are accorded sacred functions and carry the highest rank. In recent years, under the influence of increasing diffusion of Hopi concepts, the Central Plaza Kiva clans have begun to set themselves apart as the clans with the highest status. The fact that the Bear clan was once important at Walpi, that it is still important in other major Hopi villages, and that it is one of the clans of the Central Plaza Kiva group has undoubtedly strengthened this rationalization. At present, as among other major Hopi villages, the chief of Tewa Village comes from the Bear clan.

The following statement by a Bear clansman presents the situation as viewed by the Central Plaza Kiva clans:

> Our group left *c'ewadéh* ahead of the other clans. When our clans arrived at Hopi they secured a village site and farm lands and then sent for the other clans. Because our duties are sacred, we need a warrior group to defend us. Fighting an enemy must always be done with a great deal of prayer and meditation. This is as important as the actual fighting; unless our warriors are helped by war magic they will not succeed. Sometimes our magic alone is sufficient to win a victory and we do not need to sacrifice lives.

---

[58] The Hopi-Tewa view of their migration to Hopi in two groups probably reflects a former importance of a dual division in their society.

[59] According to tradition, the Hopi Snake and Bear clans asked the Hopi-Tewa to come. These clans were originally the "prestige" clans of First Mesa. The Hopi Bear clan is now extinct, and other clans—the Horn, or Flute, primarily—have assumed its duties and statuses.

The Outside Kiva clans are subject to our dictates in all important matters. In anything that pertains to the welfare of the village these clans must meet with us before they act. Their duties are concerned primarily with outside matters [secular], whereas ours pertain to religion.

A woman of the Corn clan told me that the Outside Kiva clans were "their slaves." "They do what we tell them to do. Tasks which are unpleasant, like warfare, are their responsibilities."

The Outside Kiva clans accept the Bear clan head as the Village Chief and also the notion that the Central Plaza Kiva group of clans should devote themselves to prayer and meditation. However, they emphatically deny that they were late arrivals on First Mesa. Indeed, they report that as warriors they preceded the main migration of the entire group, clearing a path and making safe the journey. They also refuse to accept the idea that clans whose functions are devoted primarily to prayer and meditation should be regarded as "better" than other clans. The report of a Cottonwood clansman expresses this point of view:

When our clans [Outside Kiva clans] left our home in the east they came directly to Hopi. This was in terms of an agreement made before the migration. Our clans were to secure a village site and farm lands and then send for the other clans. At Hopi our clans fought the enemy and then sent for the Central Plaza Kiva clans when the country had been made safe for habitation. These clans brought our sacred objects and our ceremonies, and once more we began to live as one people. There are no differences between us—we have different duties but we are the same people. We need each other to make a strong pueblo and to be effective as "protectors" of First Mesa.

It is difficult, perhaps impossible, to verify Hopi-Tewa—or Hopi—legends. Changes appear to be going on constantly to validate statuses, functions, or particular ceremonies. In the context in which the legends have been considered here, however, they are useful because they indicate quite clearly that the Hopi-Tewa are beginning to pattern their clan legends along Hopi lines.

SOCIAL CONTROL

Social control is vested primarily in two agencies—the extended family and the village as a whole. Within the family, the mother's brother—or in his absence, any adult male of the household or clan—is responsible for the maintenance of order and the discipline of younger members. The details of this process have been discussed in the section "Kinship Behavior." In the village, social control is exerted through gossip, public ridicule, social ostracism, and—at least in the past—by the charge of witchcraft. In addition, the Village Chief, the Outside Kiva Chief, the War Chief, and the Soyoku (Hopi and Hopi-Tewa bogeymen) have social control functions.

Gossip is the most common form of social control. The illustration of Hopi-Tewa reaction toward the man who began to take an active part in Hopi ceremonial life (see above, p. 293) is a good example of how gossip functions.

Public ridicule of a person who behaved improperly was formerly the special prerogative of the Koyala, or clown society. At present the society is extinct, but volunteer or appointed clowns often ridicule individuals during certain plaza dances. According to informants, the antics of the clowns today are mild, and it is said "they are afraid to make fun of town members." Instead, Navaho and whites become the subjects for ridicule.

On the occasion of a katcina dance at Tewa Village, I was once the target of the

Koyala's antics. Hopi-Tewa friends had told me many times that I smoked too much, and apparently on this occasion the Koyala had been instructed "to teach me a lesson." I was with friends, seated with my back against the wall of a house and gingerly puffing on a cigarette. The clowns climbed a house next to the one I was sitting by and then crossed over to the roof of the house directly above me. I was conscious of the presence of the clowns, but for the moment the katcina dance in the middle of the plaza occupied my attention. Then suddenly I heard the clowns yelling "Fire! Fire!" I turned to look up and caught a bucketful of water in my face. I was thoroughly drenched. The spectators laughed heartily at my discomfiture, and my hostess laughingly remarked: "Now maybe you will not smoke so much!"

A case of social ostracism and exile was reported in chapter ii, note 25. This was a typical case, I was told, though none of my informants could remember another example. A case warranting exile of an individual or family at the present time would undoubtedly be brought up for consideration by the agent or the Hopi council.

The Hopi-Tewa are reticent to discuss witchcraft. I knew of no one who was accused or suspected of witchcraft. The following general statement was obtained from a highly acculturated Hopi-Tewa man:

> People are never told that they are witches to their face. But, for example, if members of a family do not participate in ceremonies or help in the coöperative enterprises of the pueblo, they are "talked about." If anything goes wrong—if many people get sick or if it does not rain—then some people may say: "It is because that family did not help and has bad thoughts that this has happened." Soon other people will blame this family too, and then they will say about the family: "It is because they are witches and they do not want to help other people that there is so much sickness or famine." And then the family finds out about it because people "act strange." But nothing is done to the family, "they are just talked about." No one wants bad things said about him or his family, and this family will then try to help the village in work and with the ceremonies. If this family does not do this, then people will continue to think that they are witches and the family will have a hard time because "people will talk about them and act strangely toward them."

There are apparently no open accusations of witchcraft, no trials, and no executions. In this respect the Hopi-Tewa, and the Hopi too, I suspect, differ radically from the Zuni and the Indians of the Rio Grande pueblos. Witchcraft lore is enormously rich among Indians in all the pueblos except Hopi. I suspect that witchcraft gained in elaboration from Spanish contacts; as for witch hunts, trials, and executions, I believe these to be definitely of Spanish derivation. Witchcraft trials and executions fit into a Spanish or European pattern among Indians of the Rio Grande pueblos and at Zuni, where they have occurred until fairly recently.[60]

At every major ceremony the Village Chief admonishes the people to live properly. He may, at times of unusually bad behavior or in times of severe drought, send a special katcina character to both kivas, to plead for proper conduct and to urge everyone to keep a "good heart." Thus, for example, in February, 1951, a katcina impersonator representing a bear visited both kivas and warned the people against excessive drinking.

The Chief of the Outside Kiva clans tells his people to observe the admonitions of the Village Chief and lectures his group on proper behavior during the Winter Solstice ceremony. The War Chief, in the past, had the duty of maintaining order and discipline in the village. Formerly, it is reported, he had the authority to whip

---

[60] See Parsons, 1927, pp. 106–112, 125–128; Parsons, 1939, pp. 1065–1068; Scholes, 1935, pp. 218 ff.

miscreants and often exercised this right, but today the War Chief is restricted to announcing coöperative enterprises and to taking a prominent part in social dances.

Until recently, Tewa Village had a group of ogres different from the Hopi ogres called *saveyóh*.[61] The group has been replaced by the Hopi Soyoku. The War Chief designated persons to represent *saveyóh* and visit the village at certain specified times during the year. While they were about, all children were supposed to remain indoors, for these ogres were especially "fond" of children. Parents whose children needed disciplining would threaten to feed them to the monsters and would often permit their children to get a glimpse of the frightening creatures as they walked past the house.

The Hopi-Tewa have now adopted the Hopi bogeymen, or Soyoku,[62] and these impersonators appear with those of the First Mesa Hopi. Thus, about mid-morning of the day of the final Powamu night ceremony in February, the Soyoku impersonators[63] start to visit all the homes where there are children. The group spends about five to ten minutes in front of each house, peering inside and often going partly into the house. In homes in which there is a child whose behavior has been reported to them as being very bad, they pretend to try to carry off the frightened child. While this struggle is going on, other members of the group bargain with the family for a food ransom. When a satisfactory ransom has been obtained, the Soyoku move on to another home, where they repeat the performance.

The Soyoku make only one appearance a year, but parents constantly remind their children of them in order to compel obedience. The annual visits of the ogres are exceedingly traumatic experiences for the child. An acculturated Hopi-Tewa gave me the following account of his childhood recollections and reactions to the Soyoku:

When I was a little boy I wished that our house would be the first one to be visited by the Soyoku. But that never happened, for we lived almost at the other end of the village. As I heard the Soyoku coming nearer and nearer the perspiration would start running all over me. Some children cried, but I just tightened up and felt like I was going to die. My aunts[64] always came to tell me that the Soyoku would not carry me away, but my mother would say that I was very bad and that she didn't care if the Soyoku took me. When the Soyoku arrived, my aunts would fight with them to keep them away from me. My mother would bring corn meal and meat to give to the Soyoku, and she would say to me, "See how bad you've been, I have to give them all the food we have so they won't take you." That would make me feel very bad, for I felt that I was responsible for my mother giving all the food away. I would then run to my mother and grasp her dress crying: "Don't let them take me, I will be a good boy, I will work hard and get back all the food you've given to the Soyoku." Even after I was initiated and knew that the Soyoku were just ordinary people I would get frightened when I heard the noises they made.

There is an increasing disapproval of the visits of the bogeymen, particularly among wage-earning families. Another Hopi-Tewa, a government employee, de-

---

[61] According to Hopi-Tewa informants these ogres are not to be equated with the Hopi Chavaiyo (see Stephen, 1936, p. 175), nor do they resemble the Soyoku. They are reported to look like the Rio Grande Tewa *Caveyóh*, or *Cavežóh*, and to appear several times a year; not like the Soyoku who come only at Powamu. See Hill MS for a description of Rio Grande Tewa *Cavežóh*.

[62] See Fewkes, 1923, pls. 2 and 7, for pictures of the Soyoku.

[63] The two Hopi-Tewa kivas alternate in presenting the Soyoku. In February, 1950, the Outside Kiva presented them; in 1951, the Central Plaza Kiva. The Hopi-Tewa Soyoku also visit certain designated homes in Sichomovi, and the Sichomovi Soyoku visit a few homes in Tewa Village.

[64] Hopi-Tewa and First Mesa Hopi generally use the English term "aunt" when they mean father's sister.

clared that he would not permit his children to witness the activities of the Soyoku because he felt that "they were too frightening" and that his children did not need such disciplining.

The Hopi Tribal Council and Tribal Court

In 1936 the Hopi Indians adopted a tribal constitution and bylaws, formed with the aid of government specialists. The constitution (U. S. Dept. Int., 1937) authorized the establishment of a council and a court. Nine political units or voting districts were established, the division being based chiefly on the native feeling of unity among the villages. The four communities on First Mesa—Walpi, Sichomovi, Tewa Village, and Polacca—decided to work together, and thus First Mesa is considered one unit. Because the other villages were unable to reach an agreement in terms of larger groupings, each is considered a separate unit. Second Mesa forms three units: Mishongnovi, Shipolovi, and Shongopovi; Third Mesa, four units: Oraibi, New Oraibi, Hotevilla, and Bakabi; and the irrigation-farming community of Moenkopi is considered another unit.

Representation in the first Tribal Council was distributed as follows: First Mesa 4, Mishongnovi 2, Shipolovi 1, Shongopovi 2, Oraibi, 1, New Oraibi 2, Hotevilla 2, Bakabi 1, and Moenkopi 2. The officers consisted of a chairman, vice-chairman, secretary, treasurer, sergeant-at-arms, and interpreters. The duties of the Council include the regulation of tribal funds and tribal commercial enterprises; the maintenance of law and order on the reservation; the protection of tribal arts, crafts, and ceremonies; and giving of advice to the government with regard to appropriations for the benefit of the tribe.

The Council has met only sporadically since its organization and in most respects is considered a failure. Traditionally, tribal unity is foreign to the Hopi Indians. Apparently they are not ready to become organized as a tribe at the present time (see Titiev, 1944, pp. 67–68; Eggan, 1950, pp. 108–109). The Council has received support primarily from the people of First Mesa. This is true, I believe, because of the activity of the Hopi-Tewa.[65] The Hopi-Tewa's friendly and coöperative attitude toward the government and toward whites in general and their traditional role as go-betweens have helped to unite the villages of First Mesa and to convince them of the benefits that tribal unity will bring. The assumption of secular roles is "traditionally correct" for the Hopi-Tewa; the Hopi, on the other hand, disdain such roles (see Titiev, 1944, p. 67). The positions of the Hopi-Tewa as interpreters for First Mesa Hopi have already been discussed. Since the advent of the Americans, the Hopi-Tewa have also held positions as policemen. Leo Crane, a government Indian agent for the Hopi from 1911 to 1919, reports (Crane, 1925, pp. 136–137):

The Hopi do not make good policemen, and certainly not in a cohort of one. Their very name implies "the peaceful ones." Their towns are ruled largely by pueblo opinion. If a resident acquires the reputation of being unreasonable and unfeeling, as a policeman often must, his standing in the outraged community may affect all other phases of his life. Therefore the Hopi is not likely to become a very zealous officer when operating alone. And too, the Hopi fear the Navajo, as it is said the Navajo fear the Ute, and are useless when removed from the neighborhood of their homes.

But many years ago, when the Hopi were sorely pressed by nomad enemies and had not even the consolation of telling their woes to an Indian Agent, they sent emissaries to their cousins, the

---

[65] The aid of Hopi-Tewa leaders was especially helpful in the drafting of the Hopi Constitution and in "selling" the idea to the Hopi (La Farge MS).

Pueblo Indians of what is now New Mexico, and begged for a colony of warriors to reside with them. In response to this plea, and looking for something to their advantage, in 1700 came a band of the Tewa . . . To these people the Hopi granted a wide valley west of the First Mesa, known as the Wepo Wash, providing they would stay and lend their prowess in future campaigns. They built a village atop the First Mesa, now called Tewa or Hano, where their descendants live today. Some intermarried with the Hopi, and a few with the near-by Navajo; but they have not been absorbed, and it is a curious fact that while all the Tewa speak Hopi and Navajo with more or less fluency, after two centuries of living side by side few of the Hopi can speak the Tewa dialect.

The Hopi invited warriors, and the warriors have graduated into policemen, for one learns to police the Hopi districts, and even to discipline some of the Navajo, with Tewa officers. They are dependable and courageous, even belligerent; that is to say, they will fight when it is necessary and, strange thing among desert Indians, with their fists, taking a delight in blacking the opponent's eye. But one has to learn that the Hopi as policemen are fine ceremonial dancers.

This report indicates the aggressive and more independent characteristics of the Hopi-Tewa already considered. The willingness of the Hopi-Tewa to assume secular roles of responsibility, I am convinced, is the basic reason for social integration on First Mesa.

The Hopi Tribal Court follows a law-and-order code established by the Secretary of the Interior (U. S. Dept. Int., 1940, pp. 243–246). It operates independently of the Indian Service under a judge, assistant judge, and two Hopi policemen. The Hopi Tribal Court hears both Hopi and Navaho cases. Most of the cases are concerned with assaults, trespass, disorderly conduct, and driving while intoxicated. In the winter of 1950–51 I learned of only two Hopi-Tewa who appeared before the Tribal Court; they were charged with driving while intoxicated. The social control mechanisms operative within the extended household and village thus seem to be effective.

SUMMARY

Hopi-Tewa social organization reveals increasing adaptations to that of the Hopi. It is interesting, however, that in all areas non-Hopi traits persist. In the kinship system there is a retention of Tewa terms, and traces of the bilateral, generational emphasis are evident in kinship behavior. Moiety rationalizations persist in the grouping of clans and in migration legends. Social control, as with the Hopi, is restricted mainly to the household and lineage, but important controls are exercised on the village level. The most striking feature of the social organization is the increasing trend in recent years to adjust Hopi-Tewa institutions and patterns to that of the Hopi. These efforts have produced a remarkably high degree of social integration on First Mesa.

CHAPTER IV

CEREMONIAL ORGANIZATION

UNTIL RECENTLY the most pronounced difference between the Hopi-Tewa and their Hopi neighbors was in ceremonial organization. Both groups were reluctant to borrow or give up ceremonies and ritual activities. Although the kinship and clan systems were adapted comparatively early to approximate Hopi systems, the Hopi-Tewa steadfastly clung to their own unique ceremonial organization. In the past fifty or sixty years, however, there has been a pronounced breakdown of Hopi-Tewa ceremonial organization and a greater adaptation of the organization to that of the Hopi. The breakdown is due partly to the extinction of the Sun clan, but probably the most important factor is the growing acceptance by the Hopi of the Hopi-Tewa as equals.

KIVA ORGANIZATION

There are only two kivas at Tewa Village: *mu·nɛ tèh*, Central Plaza Kiva, and *p'ɛndi tèh*, Outside Kiva. Clan affiliation determines kiva membership. Members of the Bear, Corn, Tobacco, and Fir clans belong to the Central Plaza Kiva; members of the Earth, Cottonwood, and Cloud clans belong to the Outside Kiva.

It has already been mentioned that the Fir clan was formerly aligned with the Outside Kiva group of clans. At the time of the extinction of the Sun clan, or when its extinction was imminent, the Fir and Bear clans apparently seized upon a casual mention of the two clans as partners in a migration legend as an excuse to merge. The merging bolstered the membership of the Bear clan, which at the time had almost died out.[1] For the Fir clan, this linkage placed it in the prestige group of clans. The merging of the two also substituted the Fir for the Sun clan and made possible the performance of ceremonies in the Central Plaza Kiva in which four clans participated.

Formerly, the chieftainship of the village, which is also that of the chief of Central Plaza Kiva, went in turn to each of the four clans of the kiva. The last two Village Chiefs, however, have been Bear clan members; apparently their appointment was an attempt to conform to the Hopi pattern of selecting the Village Chief from that clan.[2] Reports of informants regarding the number of years a Village Chief is supposed to serve before relinquishing his office in favor of another clan are conflicting. Some reported that his term is four years, others that it is for life. All are agreed that a chief can be removed if he proves unsatisfactory; that is, if illness or drought conditions persist during his tenure.[3]

The Village Chief functions as the ceremonial head for all of Tewa Village. The

---

[1] The Bear clan was reduced to a single lineage in 1899, with only six females (Eggan, 1950, p. 169).

[2] In Stephen's time a Tobacco clansman was Village Chief (Stephen, 1936, p. 1130). Parsons remarks parenthetically that she presumes the Tobacco clansman was acting as regent for a Bear clansman (*ibid.*). It is more likely that the alternation of village chiefs among the four clans was still operative in Stephen's time. The chief of the Outside Kiva group of clans in Stephen's time was a Cottonwood clansman (see below, p. 346); today the chief is an Earth clansman A similar alternation was operative among the Outside Kiva group of clans

[3] Informants reported that if a chief proved unsatisfactory, the clan chiefs would meet and arrange his removal by simply agreeing among themselves to recognize the clan chief who would ordinarily succeed the incumbent once the latter had served his term. No other action would be taken, but public sentiment would be so strong against the chief that he would abdicate. My informants knew of no actual case of such a removal, but "had heard" of its happening in the past.

welfare of the Hopi-Tewa people is his basic concern. He is supposed to watch over his people and to succor and protect them by means of prayers for rain and for physical well-being, and he is directly responsible for the proper performance of all ceremonies. The duties of Village Chief are considered sacred, and he as a person is not supposed to take an active part in disputes or quarrels.

The Village Chief is also in charge of the Winter Solstice ceremony given by the Central Plaza Kiva. This is an annual gathering of all the men of the clans belonging to that kiva. Formerly an altar was erected, and considerable ritual was associated with the ceremony (Stephen, 1936, pp. 39–41, 49–51), but today the ceremony is comparatively simple. An altar[4] is no longer erected. It is reported that the last Winter Solstice Chief requested that all the Winter Solstice paraphernalia be buried with him. Informants relate that he was disturbed by the loss of knowledge of the proper performance of the ceremony and wanted the function discontinued after his death. Since learning the legends recited in the ceremony is extremely difficult, their disappearance is easy to understand.

The Winter Solstice ceremony has been briefly described in connection with the life cycle in the preceding chapter. A few remarks will be added here. On the final night of the ceremony, stories and clan legends are related. These tales recount the Hopi petition for Hopi-Tewa aid and tell of the hardships the Hopi-Tewa encountered after their arrival at Hopi.[5] No Hopi are admitted to this ceremony, for the stories are definitely intended to malign their hosts. Many of the legends are sung as ballads. Those recited in the Central Plaza Kiva differ in certain respects from those related in the Outside Kiva. The latter kiva has a number of war ballads, *seŋxaᵘ*, which are their own unique possessions as a warrior group. The most characteristic feature of the dance that accompanies these songs is that the men form a circle while they sing and slowly dance around a single drummer. The formation and tempo of the songs are similar to those of the Plains Indian "circle" or "round dance" songs. At regular intervals the singers emit war whoops. The songs contain refrains that tell of Hopi-Tewa bravery against the Utes, Navahos, Paiutes, and other neighboring nomadic Indian tribes, or bespeak Hopi-Tewa war magic, prowess, and the like.

Before the extinction of the Sun clan, a member of that clan functioned as Sun Watcher for all of Tewa Village. He was an assistant to the Village Chief in all important ceremonies, but also had his own duties. He was responsible for setting the time of all ceremonies in the annual Hopi-Tewa cycle, and for announcing the ceremonial dates to the village. His position was in certain respects analogous to that of the War Chief in the Outside Kiva. Both functioned as assistants and made announcements; the Sun Watcher announced items of a ceremonial nature, and the War Chief made known secular functions or instructions pertaining to war. The Hopi-Tewa now look to Walpi for the announcement of all important ceremonial dates.

The group of clans belonging to the Outside Kiva, although recognizing the ceremonial preëminence of the Central Plaza Kiva clans and accepting the Bear clan head as the Village Chief, functions in many respects as a separate and distinct

---

[4] See Fewkes, 1899, pp. 251–276, for a detailed description of Hopi-Tewa Winter Solstice altars.
[5] See "Hopi-Tewa and Hopi Relations," in chap. i, and "Land," in chap. v, for parts of the migration legend.

unit.[6] The existence of this dual division at Tewa Village has prompted Parsons (1936, pp. xliv–xlv) to speak of the situation as a survival of the Rio Grande Tewa moiety system. The Hopi-Tewa kiva groupings are in fact similar to the moiety divisions of the Rio Grande Tewa. Each group has a chief who functions separately and is said to be independent of the other. The Hopi-Tewa, like the Rio Grande Tewa, also conduct two separate initiation rites,[7] one for each group or moiety. The Hopi-Tewa organization, however, differs in that one group of clans—the Central Plaza Kiva group—is more important than the others, and the chief of Central Plaza clans is the head of the whole village. I was unable to discover whether or not ceremonial and secular responsibilities are transferred seasonally from one group to another as among the Rio Grande Tewa. Parsons (1936, p. xlv), however, reports that seasonal transfer ceremonies were still being conducted in 1920. It is not impossible that these differences between Hopi-Tewa and Rio Grande Tewa are due to the former's derivation from the Tano. Unfortunately, however, we know almost nothing about Tano culture.[8]

Formerly the Outside Kiva group consisted of the following clans: Fir, Earth, Cottonwood, and Cloud. The merging of the Fir clan and its alignment with the Central Plaza Kiva, however, leaves only three clans in the Outside Kiva. The chief[9] of this group of clans for the last fifty years has been an Earth clansman, but his predecessor was a Cottonwood clansman (Parsons, 1936, p. xliv). The succession of chiefs seems to have rotated much in the same manner as the Village Chief among the clans of the Central Plaza Kiva group.

The functions of the Outside Kiva clans are concerned, according to informants, primarily with war and secular affairs. In general, these clans, with respect to the Central Plaza Kiva clans, occupy a position analogous to that of the whole of Tewa Village with respect to Walpi. Thus the Outside Kiva clans are charged with the physical protection of the Central Plaza Kiva group. Members of the latter group are supposed to pray and go into retreat for a successful victory, but the Outside Kiva group is supposed to meet the enemy and engage it in battle. The assignment of "duties" to clans mentioned in the preceding chapter is a familiar Hopi custom. This concept may have been borrowed by the Hopi-Tewa; the duties are not assigned to individual clans, however, but to the two kiva groups.

The chief of the Outside Kiva group has an assistant called simply the War Chief, who is the head of the Cottonwood clan. I could not ascertain whether the War Chief was always a Cottonwood clansman or whether the office also formerly alternated among the four clans. The Outside Kiva Chief and the War Chief were responsible for the successful operation of a war and directed battle activities. The War Chief was charged with leading and directing periodic tribal hunts, and announced all coöperative enterprises, such as the cleaning of springs, spinning parties, working parties, and the like, for the Village Chief. Maintenance of order and discipline in the village were also responsibilities of the War Chief.

---

[6] Many informants have told me that the Central Plaza Kiva is the Summer Kiva, and the Outside Kiva the Winter Kiva; but there has been so much visiting back and forth between the Hopi-Tewa and the Rio Grande Tewa that this may be only an instance of recent borrowing.

[7] Hill (MS) has detailed descriptions of many aspects of Rio Grande Tewa (Santa Clara) social organization, from which I have drawn this information.

[8] See "Early History and Culture," in chap. i.

[9] The chief of kiva clan groups must not be confused with "Kiva Chief." A Kiva Chief is usually an old man, either a brother or an uncle of the head clanswoman of the clan that "owns" the kiva.

The main responsibility of the chief of the Outside Kiva group today, as with the Village Chief, is the Winter Solstice ceremony. This ceremony differs little from the ceremony in the Central Plaza Kiva and is held at the same time. The migration legends are different in that each group claims that it arrived before the clans of the other kiva. The Outside Kiva clans sing "war ballads": the singing of these is considered their special prerogative. The Earth clan head, who today is the chief of the Outside Kiva group of clans, still erects his altar for this ceremony.

Although membership in either kiva is determined by a person's clan affiliation, it is confirmed, for men, at the time of the Winter Solstice ceremony. At this ceremony, boys fourteen to eighteen years of age are formally inducted into the appropriate kiva.

Ownership of Tewa kivas, like that of the Hopi kivas, is ascribed to the clans that took the initiative in building them. The use of the kivas, however, is restricted to the clans believed to belong together. The Corn clan owns the Central Plaza Kiva, and the Earth clan owns the Outside Kiva. In any function for which the kiva is used, a member of the clan—usually a brother or uncle of the head clanswoman—that owns the particular kiva acts as Kiva Chief.[10]

CEREMONIES AND CEREMONIAL SOCIETIES

Until recently, the katcina cult of Tewa Village was quite different from that of the Hopi. Hopi-Tewa katcina reputedly came from a mythological lake northeast of Hopi; that is, from the "original land of the Tewa." In contrast, the "home" of the Hopi katcina is in the San Francisco Peaks near Flagstaff, Arizona, west of the Hopi villages. Two members of the Koyala, or clown society, participated and "brought" the katcina impersonators to each of the Tewa Village kivas for a one-night ceremony. There were four such katcina night ceremonies, spaced equally throughout the year. The first ceremony occurred sometime in December or January, the second in March or April, the third in July or August, and the fourth in October or November. Apparently the Hopi-Tewa katcina ceremonies have been extinct so long that the names of the ceremonies and information regarding the clans or kiva groups responsible for their performance are hopelessly confused. The December or January katcina ceremony was called *kavénah*, and the July or August ceremony, *suyukuk*ʷ*adíh*. Parsons gives *tiyogeo* as the name for the March ceremony and equates it with the Rio Grande seasonal transfer ceremony (Parsons, 1936, p. xliv). My informants did not recognize the name given by Parsons, nor that it had reference to a "transfer"; they did, however, remember a katcina ceremony celebrated in March or April. Parsons also reports an October seasonal transfer ceremony but does not give a name for it (Parsons, 1936, p. xliv). This ceremony is apparently the fourth katcina ceremony reported by my informants. I was unable to learn the names for the second and fourth katcina ceremonies.

The Hopi-Tewa katcina cult and ceremonies are obsolete; Hopi-Tewa katcina dances now follow the pattern of First Mesa as a whole and fit into the seasonal cycle directed by the Powamu society of Walpi.[11]

---

[10] The Kiva Chief receives the gifts of food that are brought by women to ceremonial participants. During the night katcina dances he obtains an ear of corn from every troupe of dancers and sprinkles sacred corn meal on all the participants. While a dance is in progress he periodically shouts approval and encouragement and may often request a performance to be repeated.

[11] The Powamu society requires each of the Hopi-Tewa kivas to select a group of katcina imper-

The Koyala, or clown society, of the Hopi-Tewa apparently was very much like the Rio Grande Tewa Kosa (*k'oʔsà·*) organization.[12] Its part in the katcina ceremony has been mentioned. In addition, the Koyala appeared in several main dances, particularly plaza dances in which large numbers participate, such as the basket or corn-grinding dances. During such a dance the clowns carried on side exhibitions for the amusement of spectators. By previous arrangement they often sought out individuals and carried them to the center of the plaza to ridicule them in view of all the spectators. The society is now extinct. Clown impersonators today are appointed only for a particular occasion and do not comprise a society.

The Shumakoli is a katcina curing society[13] now controlled by the Cloud clan, although formerly it belonged to the extinct Sun clan. The society cures "sore eyes"; but any Hopi-Tewa or even a Hopi from First Mesa may request the society to dance, either to effect a personal cure or to secure well-being for the community in general. A ceremony is held in August or September, in which the society inducts new members. Members are drawn from both Hopi and Hopi-Tewa communities. Since the Cloud clan is almost extinct, I was told that the society will probably die out with the death of the old Cloud clansman who is at present head of the society.

Members for Hopi-Tewa ceremonial societies are recruited in the same manner as for the Rio Grande Tewa societies: by vow of parents before the birth of a child, by vow of either a severely ill person or his parents, or by trespass into an area enclosed by a line of meal where the particular society has erected its altar for its annual or major ceremony. In addition, entrance may be purely voluntary, as among the Hopi. In each case a ceremonial sponsor is selected in the manner described in the preceding chapter.

In addition to established societies for curing, there are individual Hopi-Tewa shamans, or doctors. These have a good practice, not only among the Hopi-Tewa but among the Hopi of all the mesas and the Navaho as well. Hopi-Tewa shamans are respected and renowned for their successful healing practices. Undoubtedly they have this reputation because of their Rio Grande ancestry;[14] the Hopi and Navaho both have a deep respect for Rio Grande Pueblo shamans.

The Winter Solstice ceremony, or *θàŋ θaⁱ*, has already been discussed. Actually there are two such ceremonies, one in each kiva, conducted independently of the other, though they take place on the same day and coincide as well with the final night of the Soyala, or Winter Solstice ceremony, of the Hopi at Walpi. Before the position of Sun Watcher lapsed, it is reported, the Hopi-Tewa chose their own time to hold the solstice ceremonies, and this was not necessarily the same as the final night of the Hopi Soyala.

Other Hopi-Tewa ceremonies have apparently lapsed. There is no longer a Summer Solstice ceremony, though Parsons reported it in 1920 (Parsons, 1936, p. xliv).

sonators who perform first in their own kiva and then visit in turn all the other eight kivas on First Mesa. The present katcina initiation ceremonies, although performed by the Hopi-Tewa Central Plaza Kiva, are identical with those of the Hopi at Walpi, as far as my informants knew. All reported that both the present cult and initiations are recent; they did not know what took place in the earlier cult initiations, although they believed that they were quite different.

[12] Hill (MS on Santa Clara Pueblo) has excellent descriptions of the Rio Grande Tewa Kosa.

[13] Stephen (1936, pp. 818–823) describes a Shumakoli ceremony in detail.

[14] Hopi and Navaho have long recognized the curing powers of the Rio Grande Pueblo Indians. For references to the curing emphasis of Rio Grande Pueblo ceremonial organizations, see Hawley, 1937, p. 504; Eggan, 1950, pp. 172–173.

At any time during the year, the chief of the Central Plaza Kiva or the chief of the Outside Kiva may gather the men of his kiva to engage in prayer-stick making, but this does not occur at any specified time in the annual cycle. Prayer sticks are made and deposited in order to bring rain or to insure good health. Such activities start in early morning and are usually finished by mid-afternoon, when the prayer sticks are taken by one or two men to be deposited in the various Hopi-Tewa shrines and in the springs that belong to Tewa Village.[15]

INITIATION

Hopi-Tewa initiation into the katcina cult today is almost identical with that of the Hopi.[16] All Hopi-Tewa are eventually initiated into the cult. (For a detailed description of katcina initiation, see "The Life Cycle" in the preceding chapter.) Only the Central Plaza Kiva is empowered to conduct katcina initiations; members of clans of the Outside Kiva must come to the Central Plaza Kiva to be initiated.[17]

Initiation, or induction, into a kiva group is uniquely Hopi-Tewa; the Hopi do not have kiva initiation. This initiation is only for men and is the closest approach the Hopi-Tewa have to the elaborate Hopi tribal initiation.[18] Hopi-Tewa kiva initiations suggest the moiety initiations of the Rio Grande Tewa but differ from them in certain essential features. Thus the Rio Grande Tewa moiety initiations are elaborate affairs and induct both men and women (see Hill MS), whereas the Hopi-Tewa rites are simple rituals and are restricted to men. All Bear, Fir, Tobacco, and Corn clansmen between fourteen and eighteen years of age are inducted into the Central Plaza Kiva; young men of corresponding ages belonging to the Earth, Cottonwood, and Cloud clans are inducted into the Outside Kiva. In early times the initiation may have been more complex (see Parsons, 1926, p. 212), but today the initiates merely attend the final night of the Winter Solstice ceremony with their ceremonial fathers. The inductees receive a new name from their ceremonial fathers and may thereafter attend all important functions of their kiva.

Katcina and kiva initiations (induction at the Winter Solstice ceremony) appear to be reversed when compared with similar Rio Grande Tewa ceremonies. Katcina initiations among the Rio Grande Tewa are restricted to boys and occur sometime after the boy is fourteen years of age; moiety initiations, however, which confirm membership into one of two groups, induct children of both sexes of an age comparable to those of Hopi-Tewa children inducted into the katcina cult.[19]

The present Village Chief, from whom I obtained the major part of the information presented in this chapter, made the following statement about the present status of ceremonial life at Tewa Village:

When the Sun clan people were still with us, Tewa Village was like a separate pueblo. We were not bound by the ceremonial dictates of the Walpi leaders. Our Sun clan determined the position of the sun and the phases of the moon. Without recourse to Walpi we started our own prayer-stick

[15] See Stephen, 1936, p. 392, for a detailed account of Hopi-Tewa prayer-stick making.

[16] Voth has given a detailed description of Hopi katcina initiation in Oraibi (Voth, 1901). Stephen (1936, pp. 198–203) gives an excellent description of a katcina initiation on First Mesa in 1893.

[17] I could find no informant that could tell me about earlier katcina initiation rites, i.e., before the Hopi-Tewa adopted the Hopi types.

[18] The complex Hopi tribal initiation ceremonies have been described in detail by Titiev, 1944, chap. x.

[19] Rio Grande Tewa appear to be quite uniform in ceremonial organization. The initiation rites referred to here are specifically those of Santa Clara Pueblo (Hill MS).

making in the kivas and celebrated our private and public ceremonies separately from Walpi. It is true that in those days there was bad feeling between Hopi and Hopi-Tewa, but we were strong then and we did not mind what the Hopi thought about us. Now I have to wait until the Walpi chief has announced *Soyala* [the Hopi Winter Solstice ceremony] before I can go into the kiva at θàη θaˁ [Hopi-Tewa Winter Solstice ceremony].[20] This is true of all other ceremonies that we have—before we start them we must consult with Walpi. When I was a youth my grandmother and my granduncles used to tell me that the Hopi did not like us to hold separate ceremonies—they accused the Hopi-Tewa of "playing around with their wives" while they were in retreat. When the Sun clan became extinct and the office of Sun Watcher disappeared with it, we had to give in to the Hopi. Since that time we have been slowly losing our ceremonies, and my position as Tewa Village Chief is no longer as important as it was in my grandparents' generation. My hands are bound, I can act in ceremonial matters only with the approval of the Walpi chief. We may all become Hopi some day, but I keep telling the young men at θàη θaˁ what is my responsibility as Village Chief. That is, to impress upon all of us that we are Tewa and different from the Hopi and that we must always remember this. The young people do not take these things seriously, but it is my duty to tell them.

The present Village Chief has little influence or power. Indeed, he is not even held in high esteem; as remarked previously, the Hopi-Tewa interpreter enjoys greater respect and prestige. It would seem, therefore, that with the disappearance of Hopi-Tewa ceremonial life, secular positions will become increasingly important for the Hopi-Tewa. Hopi ceremonial organizations have already made considerable headway into Hopi-Tewa society and will probably eventually displace the earlier system. First Mesa appears to be moving toward an integration that will be characterized by a rich Hopi ceremonialism and a high degree of political cohesion achieved through the secular interests of the Hopi-Tewa.

RITUAL ACTIVITIES TODAY

Since the Hopi-Tewa have permitted many of their own ritual activities to lapse, they now coöperate in various ways to keep First Mesa Hopi ceremonies operating efficiently within the annual ceremonial calendar.[21] However, only in terms of the katcina cult, which is organized, like that of the Hopi, in kiva groups, do the Hopi-Tewa actually participate in Hopi ceremonial life.[22] As participants in the katcina cult, the Hopi-Tewa are wholly under the direction and supervision of the Powamu society. Although the Hopi-Tewa are permitted to choose the katcina characters they impersonate,[23] they must synchronize their performances to correspond with those of all the other kiva groups on First Mesa. There are nine kivas on First Mesa, including those of Tewa Village, and each has a katcina group.[24] Katcina dances start with the Powamu ceremony[25] in February and end with the Niman, or "home-

---

[20] The dates of the major Hopi and Hopi-Tewa ceremonies are determined eight or sixteen days before the event occurs. The Tewa Village Chief is notified by Walpi leaders when he can start his ceremonies.

[21] Parsons, 1939, pp. 501–514, has described the First Mesa ceremonial calendar in full. The description is still valid for the katcina cycle in which the Hopi-Tewa participate today.

[22] Except for the very few Hopi-Tewa who belong to Hopi ceremonial societies. See note 30, below.

[23] There are many kinds of katcina characters and many impersonators of each. Stephen (1936, pp. 1137–1152) gives 150 types. Katcina dancers may be all of one kind, paired, or of mixed types. The number of dancers usually varies with the number of men in a particular kiva—the usual number being between 20 and 30.

[24] Soon after a boy is initiated into the katcina cult—when he is eight to ten years old—he may participate in his kiva as a katcina dancer.

[25] Theoretically, katcina impersonators may appear at the Winter Solstice ceremony, but in practice they first appear at the Powamu ceremony.

going," ceremony in July. Each kiva group presents its own dance without consulting any of the other groups.[26] Spectators go into any one of the nine First Mesa kivas—usually the one nearest to home—to see all nine performances, since each kiva group starts in its own kiva and then visits all the other eight kivas successively. In February and March, katcina performances are held inside the kiva and occur weekly on Saturday nights.[27] From April until the end of the katcina season, the dances are less frequent and are usually given outdoors in the village plazas.

The Niman, a Hopi ceremony, occurs in mid- or late July and marks the return of the katcinas to their home in the San Francisco Mountains, according to Hopi belief. During the rest of the year until the following Powamu no masked or katcina dances are permitted by the Hopi. In the past the Hopi-Tewa frequently violated this mandate and provoked much ill feeling. There are still occasional infractions by the Hopi-Tewa, such as the appearance of the Shumakoli katcina in August or September and an occasional "social dance" in the katcina season, when such dances are prohibited. But such violations are becoming less and less frequent with the loss of strictly Hopi-Tewa ceremonies and the increasing desire of the Hopi-Tewa to coöperate with the Hopi and to appear favorably in their eyes.

The end of the First Mesa katcina season terminates the active participation of the Hopi-Tewa in ceremonial activities.[28] During the rest of the year the Hopi-Tewa assist the Hopi with their ceremonies and act as hosts along with their neighbors for all visitors to First Mesa. Hopi-Tewa women work industriously in the preparation of food for their Hopi husbands and for other Hopi relatives who are actively engaged in these ceremonies. The men perform various services for their Hopi kinsmen. All share in the festive occasions and open their houses to all visitors.

During that part of the year when katcina dances are forbidden and the katcina are reportedly away in the San Francisco Peaks, the Hopi-Tewa give frequent "social dances."[29] Usually only a small group of unmarried men and women participate in these dances. Many of the dances have been borrowed from other tribes, usually from the Rio Grande Tewa. In these dances there are many attempts to introduce the war theme. As the dancers emerge from the kiva, Plains war-dance songs are sung. The War Chief dons his best war costume and periodically emits an ear-splitting war whoop. The men also try to appear like their Rio Grande Tewa kinsmen by braiding their hair or by wearing false braids. Today many Rio Grande Tewa journey to Hopi in order to teach the Hopi-Tewa new songs and dances and to appear with them in the dances. The Hopi-Tewa in turn make frequent visits to the Rio Grande areas.

For arranging all the social dances for one year—excluding those in the regular cycle—two men are chosen from each kiva group to act as supervisors. Their duties consist of collecting all the needed paraphernalia, choosing a drummer, selecting the girls who are to dance, and assisting the dancers to put on their costumes and

---

[26] The Hopi and Hopi-Tewa delight in surprises. Innovations in katcina types are also common; many of the types now popular have recently been introduced by the Hopi-Tewa.

[27] Saturday night katcina dances are a recent adjustment to employment and schooling.

[28] Except for the Shumakoli ceremony in August or September and the Winter Solstice ceremony given in mid-December.

[29] The Hopi of First Mesa also give social dances in the season when there are no katcina dances, but the Hopi-Tewa dances are most frequent and most varied. Examples of "social dances" are the Buffalo, *O hoiki*, and *Yandewa* dances. Parsons, 1923, pp. 21–26, has described the Buffalo dance in detail.

make-up before each appearance. In addition, they see that the kiva is in proper order and that sufficient wood is brought to keep the place warm for rehearsals and for the final day of the dance.

A dance of the Rio Grande Tewa called *pą́ŋšaréh* by the Tewa and *Panchale* by the Hopi has become increasingly popular on First Mesa in recent years. Panchale has apparently no religious significance. It has some resemblance to white American social dancing, but the Rio Grande Tewa claim that it is old and native with them. Boys choose girls (sometimes there are "lady's choice" dances as well!), and about ten or more couples dance to the beat of a drum and a chorus of singers. A song and dance has several sets similar to the Virginia Reel. One complete dance with its series of variations lasts for about fifteen minutes. The tempo is lively and a round of dancing leaves the young dancers breathless and flushed.

I was told that the Hopi objected to the dance when it was introduced, about twenty years ago, on the ground that it was "not Indian." Panchale is extremely popular on First Mesa today, however, although it is not danced during the katcina season and, so far as I know, it is danced nowhere else on the Hopi reservation but in Tewa Village. Young Hopi and Hopi-Tewa boys and girls are enthusiastic about Panchale and come from other villages to join in.

SUMMARY

Before 1900, the Hopi-Tewa and the Hopi were pronouncedly distinct in ceremonial organization. The present kiva organization, society, and ceremonial ritual, despite surface similarities, indicate differences that were undoubtedly sharper at an earlier period. Initiation into the katcina cult now, however, is almost identical with that of the Hopi. Here is undoubtedly evidence that with the disappearance of their own katcina cult, the Hopi-Tewa have adopted the katcina practices of the Hopi. Unfortunately, I was unable to obtain information about initiation into their own type of katcina cult at an earlier period in Hopi-Tewa history. Adaptation to the Hopi katcina cycle seems to have completely replaced the earlier cult and the ceremonial cycle consonant with it. Kiva initiations, however, remain uniquely Hopi-Tewa. They resemble the Rio Grande Tewa moiety initiations on the one hand, and the Hopi tribal initiations on the other. The elaborate ritual practices of both Rio Grande Tewa and Hopi, however, contrast sharply with the simple, one-night ceremony of the Hopi-Tewa.

Today the Hopi-Tewa participate unreservedly and wholeheartedly in the First Mesa katcina cycle. At other times of the year they engage enthusiastically in social dances. Although they rarely join Hopi societies[30] they coöperate with the Hopi in all their ceremonial activities and, with their neighbors, act as hosts to all visitors.

[30] Only thirteen men are members of the all-important Hopi tribal men's society; none joined in the last initiation held in November, 1950. Initiations into this society are held every four or five years. Only three men are members of the Powamu society. Four women are members of the Hopi Mamzrau society.

CHAPTER V

ECONOMICS

THE HOPI-TEWA, like their Hopi neighbors, are still basically horticulturists. Livestock and wage work, however, have become increasingly important in recent years. These economic activities are potential threats to the integrity of the clan structure and may stimulate a social reorganization. But at present, the Hopi-Tewa, as well as the Hopi of First Mesa generally, are handling the new economic pursuits largely in terms of traditional experience. Sharing of work and food within the extended household, clan, and phratry have helped to prevent a permanent segmentation of the society into nuclear family units. Although a family that has wage workers or sheep and cattle may live as a nuclear family for long periods, it reverts to extended-family living and assumes clan responsibilities once it is back in Tewa Village or in Polacca. These fluctuations between nuclear-family and extended-household living and the participation in clan responsibilities and privileges occur with great frequency. With families owning sheep and cattle, these fluctuations are usually seasonal: nuclear-family living in the summer, extended-household living in the winter. The families who are engaged in wage work at Keams Canyon revert to extended-household living on week ends. The rich Hopi-Tewa social and ceremonial calendar also brings back nuclear-family units to participate as extended-household units and to resume clan duties and responsibilities.

The practice of sharing food and work has also prevented economic stratification; that is, there are no pronounced differences between poor and wealthy families. Sharing of food and the exchange of services within the household, clan, phratry, kiva groups, and community have provided for distributions which essentially place the whole population on an equal economic footing.

LAND

The Hopi-Tewa report that in exchange for the services they rendered as "warriors" and "protectors" of the Hopi on First Mesa they were given lands extending northward from this mesa (see map 4). According to the Hopi-Tewa, one of the primary inducements for coming to Hopi was the offer of assertedly productive land. The migration legend annually recited in the Hopi-Tewa kivas at the time of the Winter Solstice, reports in part:

Four times the Walpi Bear Clan Chief and Snake Clan Chief came to our village at c'ę·wadéh. They brought with them prayer sticks that represented the things that would be given to us if we would come and fight their enemies. There was one for the women that were promised to our men; there was one for the village site that we would occupy; there was one for the springs from which we would obtain our drinking water; there was one for the land on which we could raise our corn and other crops . . . They drew for us on the sand the large stalks of corn that were raised on the land that would be ours. They extended both arms to indicate the size of the ears of corn that grew on this land. "All this will be yours if you will come and live among us as our protectors," they said. "In our land you will have plenty to eat and your storehouses will always be full."

Hopi-Tewa like to relate how shamefully their forefathers were deceived by the Hopi. The land was poor, and no amount of hard work could make it produce the crops they were promised. Their storehouses were often empty, and they suffered

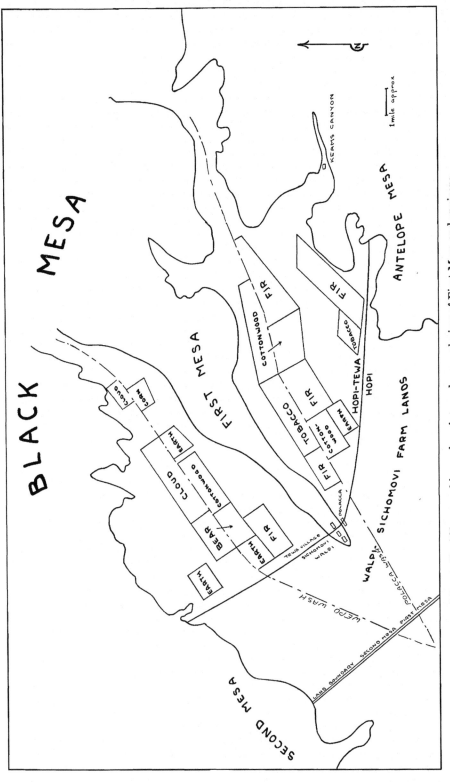

Map 4. Hopi-Tewa arable garden plots and general view of First Mesa and environs.

through the drought-stricken years. But the Hopi-Tewa, like the Hopi, learned to overcome the rigors of the environment.

The Hopi reservation poses many difficult problems for farming.[1] Only by ingenious and arduous methods of planting and caring for their growing crops have the Hopi and Hopi-Tewa garnered a living from the land.[2] The rainfall is scant, averaging only about ten inches per year. The altitude of 6,000 to 6,500 feet brings early and late frosts that limit the growing season to barely three months. In July and August sudden cloudbursts are common and cause considerable damage. To insure a crop against these odds, a Hopi-Tewa farmer plants two or three fields, which he chooses with great care. Kirk Bryan's observation of Hopi-planted fields is applicable to the Hopi-Tewa (Bryan, 1929, p. 445):

> The areas utilized are variable in size and location, but each is chosen so that the local rainfall may be reinforced by the overflow of water derived from higher ground. The selection of a field involves an intimate knowledge of local conditions. The field must be flooded, but the sheet of water must not attain such velocity as to wash out the crop nor carry such a load of detritus as to bury the growing plants. Such conditions require a nice balance of forces that occur only under special conditions. Shrewd observation and good judgment are necessary in the selection of fields.

OWNERSHIP AND INHERITANCE

There have been some changes recently in ownership and inheritance,[3] but in general the pattern is still much as it was in earlier times.

Clan plots are allotted within the land area traditionally assigned to the Hopi-Tewa. Hopi-Tewa lands extend north of the Tewa Village–Sichomovi boundary line. This boundary line extends west across the Wepo wash and east across the Polacca wash (see map 4). Clan boundaries are set off by stone symbols marked to represent the various clans and placed along sight lines. Within a clan plot, the mother of each family has several fields at her disposal. When her daughters marry, a woman gives each of them one or more plots of land, or parts of several. Upon her death, female matrilineal relatives assume control of the land, the direct descendants having prior claim. The question of disposal of lands to married daughters has often little practical importance since the daughters continue to live in the house and with the family of the mother.[4]

Men have no right to ownership or inheritance of land; they work it, however. When a man marries, he relinquishes his right to work on his own clan lands and works on his wife's. Before he marries, a young man works on his own clan lands, and he may return to them in the event of a separation or a divorce. The farm hands in

---

[1] An exhaustive treatment of the relationship of the Hopi to their physical environment has been given by Hack, 1942. Forde (1931) discusses Hopi farming chiefly from the point of view of Hopi-Tewa informants.

[2] Stewart (1940, pp. 329–335) gives an excellent account of Hopi flood farming and the methods used by the Hopi.

[3] Ownership and inheritance patterns described by Forde (1931, pp. 366–383) for First Mesa Hopi parallel Hopi-Tewa patterns in all essential features. The differences between the present and the former patterns are due to modern changes; cash income from livestock sales and wage work has increased individual property. Formerly a man had only a few possessions he could call his own; now he often has money and buys numerous articles. Property acquired by a man in this way is usually inherited by his sons or is specifically transmitted to certain persons before his death.

[4] In recent years a new trend appears to have been established: the girl's male household members build another house for the couple on the girl's clan plots at Polacca. Such a house may not be built for several years, however, and during that time the couple lives in the girl's maternal house and no assignment of farming land is made specifically for the couple.

a typical Hopi-Tewa extended household include a woman's father, her unmarried maternal uncles, her bachelor brothers, her husband, her unmarried sons, and the husbands of her sisters.[5]

Houses and household equipment, like land, are owned and inherited in the female line within a clan. A woman may give certain sections of her house for the use of one of her daughters when she marries, or with the help of men of her family—her husband, brothers, sons—she may erect a new house for the couple, or an addition to the old one, or she may simply receive her son-in-law into her own house. All the furnishings and equipment within a house also belong to the senior woman of the household; a man owns only the clothes and jewelry that are on his person.

In contrast to land and houses, horses, cattle, and sheep are the property of men. When a man marries or divorces, he takes his own personal flock or herd with him. The care of sheep and care of cattle are male occupations. Although a woman may often inherit or acquire shares in flocks, her husband or one of her male relatives is given the task of caring for them (see "Sharing within the Household," below).

ECONOMIC ACTIVITIES

Before economic activities are discussed, the coöperative nature of Hopi-Tewa society should be made clear. Marriage and kinship ties and the economic responsibilities involved in these relationships interrelate the whole community. These patterns cannot be adequately described by a discussion of economic activities alone. The conventional economic analysis, liberally supplied with statistical tables indicating per capita or family incomes, may have meaning in our society but blur the true economic picture of a highly coöperative society such as that of the Hopi or Hopi-Tewa. For the purpose of clarifying the picture, a section on coöperative enterprises has been included after the discussion of economic activities.

Economic activities are described in terms of adult individuals. This is because the available records kept by the Hopi Indian Agency are in terms of individuals. Another reason is that, although the household is the basic unit of production and consumption, it is an extremely fluctuating unit, the size and composition of which are difficult to determine at any one time. Added to this are the instability of the population and the frequent social and ceremonial occasions that bring together larger segments of the population.

Basic data on economic activity are presented in three tables: table 4, "Estimated Annual Income of Government Wage Workers and Livestock Owners"; table 5, "Ownership of Cattle and Sheep"; and table 6, "Primary Economic Activities of Employable Persons."

Most of the Hopi-Tewa wage income comes from employment at the Hopi Agency, in Keams Canyon, twelve miles from First Mesa. Employment by the government is of two general types, permanent and irregular (table 4). There were eleven persons (two of whom were women) who were engaged in permanent government employment in 1950–1951, earning an estimated annual income of $29,700. Permanent government positions range from cook, with an annual salary of $2,252.00, to that of interpreter, with an annual salary of $3,950.00. For nine of the eleven permanent government employees, government quarters were provided for the workers at

---

[5] This is not true in households where wage work and (or) livestock activities are of major importance; in these the number of men engaged in horticultural activities is much smaller.

Keams Canyon. These quarters rent at a low rate—as low as $5.00 per month—but are in general inferior to the village homes of the employees.

There were sixteen Hopi-Tewa who were employed in irregular government employment in 1950–1951, and their combined estimated annual income was $28,800 (table 4).[6] The majority of the jobs under irregular government employment are unskilled. None of these employees are provided with government quarters.

CATTLE AND SHEEP

Twenty-two persons owned a total of 658 head of cattle in 1950 and twenty-one owned a total of 1,602 sheep (see table 5). About one-fourth of the total livestock is sold each year. In the fall of 1950, the Hopi Indian Agency's estimated values of

TABLE 4
ESTIMATED ANNUAL INCOME OF GOVERNMENT WAGE WORKERS AND LIVESTOCK OWNERS
(From Hopi Indian Agency Records, 1951)

	Men	Women	Estimated annual income (in $1,000's)
Permanent government employment.	9	2	29 7
Irregular employment	16	0	28 8
Owning flocks of sheep . .	22	0	5 0
Owning cattle	° 21	0	17 1
Totals..	68	2	80 6

TABLE 5
OWNERSHIP OF CATTLE AND SHEEP
(From Hopi Indian Agency Records, 1951)

Livestock	Number of owners	Total cattle or sheep owned
Sheep . .	22	1,602
Cattle . . .	21	658

sheep and cattle were $12.50 and $104.00 a head, respectively. On the basis of these estimated values, persons contributing to Hopi-Tewa support realized an income of $5,000 from sheep sales and $17,100 from cattle sales in 1950 (see table 4).

TOTAL CASH INCOME

The estimated annual cash income from government employment and livestock sales was $80,600 (table 4). In addition, there were other sources of cash income, such as nongovernment employment, compensations to servicemen's dependents, Social Security benefits, relief obtained from the Indian Service, and arts and crafts (particularly pottery)—amounting to an additional $20,000. The total annual income amounted roughly to $100,000 in 1950–1951.[7]

[6] Irregular government employment has been computed on an annual basis. Several payrolls for 1950–1951 were examined. During this time there was some turnover in personnel, but the number engaged in irregular employment remained substantially the same for each year.

[7] Annual per capita Hopi-Tewa cash income amounts to about $250.00.

HORTICULTURE

The importance of horticulture is difficult to present in terms of figures and statistical tables. The foregoing discussion of wage work and livestock activities tends to give these occupations greater importance than they deserve. As a cash income, horticulture is negligible, but Hopi-Tewa crops still furnish the basic subsistence for the people. Agency records were of little help in providing an index to the importance of horticulture. Acreage of planted crops was not listed for the Hopi-Tewa specifically. For First Mesa in 1950, the Hopi Indian Agency records the number of acres planted, as follows: beans 63, melons 108, garden products 110 (21 acres irrigated), and corn 870 acres. It is safe to say that at least one-third of this acreage was farmed by Hopi-Tewa.

The central position of horticulture in Hopi-Tewa culture is revealed by the customs and activities of the people. Ritually, Hopi-Tewa society, like all pueblo societies, revolves around horticulture. All ceremonies have as their main theme the propitiation of the spirits so that they will make the crops bountiful. It is not only in religion, however, but also in secular activities that horticulture is stressed. From spring to fall the Hopi-Tewa are in the fields, working to produce crops from an inhospitable environment. Harvesttime is a period of feasting and gaiety. Everyone is happy and all generously give the fruits of the land to visitors. At this time large numbers of Navaho come to the village to avail themselves of the food given generously by their hosts.

In the summer of 1949 I lived for two weeks on a farm with part of a Hopi-Tewa household consisting of husband, wife, son, daughter, the wife's two brothers, her male cousin, and the cousin's son. The men worked several hours each day on their fields and crops—making fence repairs, hoeing, covering young plants with tin cans or placing dirt around them to prevent strong winds from blowing the plants away, and making shallow ditches and borders to divert rain and floodwaters to the crops. After a rain they would go immediately to observe its effects and to see whether any of the plants had been damaged by flood and silt. While I was living with this family on their farm I also had the opportunity to observe neighboring Hopi-Tewa families who similarly devoted long hours of meticulous labor and care to their crops.

PRIMARY OCCUPATIONS

Table 6 gives a summary of the primary economic activities of all persons nineteen years of age and above. This table gives the following information: 43 livestock owners, 27 government employees, 18 persons employed off the reservation, 13 farmers at Parker, 50 occupied with horticulture at Hopi, and 52 workers engaged in handicrafts.

From this table we see that more than one-half of all persons nineteen years of age and above are still engaged in horticulture or in handicrafts (115 out of 203). The 88 livestock owners and wage workers are also, of course, periodically occupied with farming, and all share in farm produce.[8] It is therefore evident that the traditional economic activities of the Hopi-Tewa are still basic to the people. It is also

---

[8] It is important to emphasize that there is a great deal of overlap in economic activity, that is, almost all men work for wages periodically and (or) have sheep and cattle. All women make pottery and do housework; in addition, many of them work occasionally for the government. Table 6 thus lists only *primary* economic activities.

clear, however, that livestock raising and wage work are crucial aspects of the Hopi-Tewa economy, and it is doubtful whether the Hopi-Tewa could subsist on horticulture alone.

TABLE 6

PRIMARY ECONOMIC ACTIVITIES OF EMPLOYABLE PERSONS

Ages nineteen years and above, except the very old

(From Hopi Indian Agency records, my census data, and information supplied by informants)

	Primary economic activity	Men	Women	Totals
Cash operation	Livestock owners	43	0	43
	Government employment	25	2	27
	Employed off reservation	10	8	18
	Totals	78	10	88
Subsistence and handicraft	Farming at Parker[a]	7	6	13
	Horticulture on reservation	50	0	50
	Handicraft (pottery, tanning, weaving)	25	27	52
	Totals	82	33	115
	Total engaged			203

[a] Parker, Arizona—an area of irrigated farmlands on the Colorado River recently made available to Hopi, Navaho, and other Southwestern Indians.

COÖPERATIVE ENTERPRISES

The household functions constantly as an economic unit; its members assist one another in daily duties and see that all are properly fed and clothed. Food sharing and the exchange of services in larger units of the society operate in relation to the social and ceremonial functions, which occur with remarkable frequency and regularity. A quick review of such functions that occurred in 1950 is worth while here. In the month of January there were seven weddings and two social dances; from February to May there were weekly katcina dances. June and July were busy months in the field; but there was one social dance and a water-spring cleaning job in June, and in mid-July the Hopi-Tewa joined the Hopi with their Niman festivities. August was an occasion for another social dance, two more weddings, and the Hopi Snake Dance. In September and October the Hopi-Tewa were busy with harvest; but a Shumakoli ceremony was celebrated in mid-September, and in late October the complex tribal initiation ceremonies began at Walpi.

Social and ceremonial functions have a leveling effect and prevent the segmentation of the population into rich and poor. Money as such is not contributed or divided; it is food—including tobacco and cigarettes—that is distributed. This food is either home grown (that is, farm produce and livestock products) or it is bought in trading posts or off-reservation towns for the purpose of distribution. Hopi-Tewa culture prescribes that everyone should give generously, and the givers expend much effort to donate large amounts. Since production and income derived from wage work, livestock, handicrafts, and other sources vary among the households, the amount of food given is not the same from each household. Division of the food among the receivers, however, is *equal*, and this has a leveling effect. The kind of social or ceremonial function determines who is to give and who is to receive. In certain functions—a wedding, for example—those benefiting from food gifts are essentially restricted to the bridegroom's clan and phratry, whereas the givers are mainly members of the bride's clan and phratry.[9] In a kiva group ceremony, such as a social dance or a katcina dance, the members of the group of clans that belong to the particular kiva sponsoring the ceremony are both givers and receivers. Such a function operates in the following manner. Women belonging to these clans carry the food to the kiva, and the men of the clans receive it. The food is divided equally by the kiva chief and his assistants among all the men participating in the ceremony. When the food has been divided, it is taken by the men to their respective households. A man will thus take back some of the food contributed by members of his own household, but he will also have some of the food contributed by all the other households. Hence a variety of food products is taken back. As a rule, those households contributing more will receive less, and those giving little will receive more.

Ceremonial functions in larger units operate in much the same manner as has been outlined above for the kiva group. Food in coöperative operations of this sort is also contributed by women and is divided equally in the kiva or kivas by the men and taken back to their respective households when the ceremonies are over.

In connection with these coöperative enterprises, work has to be done. The givers buy groceries, butcher cattle and sheep, prepare food, and carry it to the kivas. The receivers are also constantly working either in prayer or in the many tasks required to make the particular ceremony successful. All such work is done coöperatively, with gaiety and good fellowship.

The sharing of food and exchange of services, as noted previously, operates through specific social and ceremonial customs in a hierarchy of units: clan, kiva group, community, and the whole of First Mesa.[10] Illustrations of the kind of activity involved in each one of these coöperative enterprises is described in the following pages. The household, though not dependent on social and ceremonial functions, is described first because it is the crucial economic unit.

SHARING WITHIN THE HOUSEHOLD

In discussing the problem of food sharing and the exchange of services within the household, I have selected one more or less typical unit to illustrate the economic activities. This household belongs to the Corn clan and consists of an old Hopi-Tewa couple, their two daughters who are married to Hopi men, and their children. The relationship is shown in fig. 4; the names used are fictitious.

For indefinite periods this extended family lives separately in three family units: Paul and Edith, the old couple, live by themselves in an old house at Tewa Village; Marie, their younger daughter, and her husband Peter and their children live in a

---

[9] Father's sisters also contribute food for their brother's daughter's marriage, as do the ceremonial mothers of the girl.

[10] Beaglehole (1937, pp. 27–28) describes a similar hierarchical pattern of coöperative enterprises in Second Mesa villages.

separate house, also at Tewa Village; and the older daughter, Josie, who works as a cook at the Hopi Indian Agency, lives with her husband, John, and their children in government quarters at Keams Canyon. In the summertime Paul and Edith move to their ranch house, where Paul tends his sheep and cattle, assisted by a brother and often by other male members of the Corn clan. Two or more of the grandchildren are usually with the old couple on the ranch.

In the summertime, the nuclear family of the two daughters is thus reduced, with some of their children living on the ranch of the old couple. The younger daughter remains on the mesa top with her young children; the older daughter

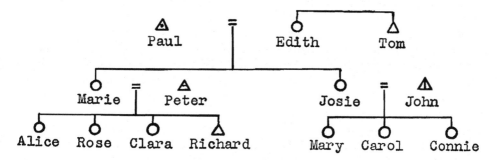

O △   Hopi-Tewa Corn clan

△   A different Hopi-Tewa clan

△   A Hopi clan

△   A second Hopi clan

Fig. 4. A Hopi-Tewa household. Tom is married to a Walpi woman and belongs to a different household; he has no economic relations in his sister's household. He frequently visits his sister, however, and she consults with him in important ritual matters and refers to him all difficult cases of disciplining her children and grandchildren.

continues with her regular job at Keams Canyon, assisted in household chores by her older daughter, while her younger daughters spend the summer at the ranch.

During the summer months, John and Peter, Josie's and Marie's husbands, respectively, farm a portion of the Corn clan lands belonging to their mother-in-law, Edith. Paul, when not busy with his cattle and sheep, gives his sons-in-law a hand with their farming activities, and in return they often help him with his livestock. John and Peter also are irregularly employed by the government and engage in wage-work activities sporadically. Both Hopi husbands also help their own Hopi clan relatives who own cattle and sheep.

In the winter, the situation changes somewhat. Although Keams Canyon is twelve miles from First Mesa, Josie comes with her husband and children every week end to spend Saturday and Sunday with her parents. Since Marie and Peter and their children live at Tewa Village, they are constantly visiting with the old couple and exchanging services with them. In the winter, as in the summer, the Hopi men are periodically on the government payroll. John works irregularly as a stonemason, and Peter occasionally works for the Indian Agency as a day laborer. John and Peter have no cattle and sheep, but some of their clansfolk have some, and John and Peter often assist them in herding activities.

Marie and Josie on their frequent visits to their parents bring food, either from their stores of gardening produce or from the trading posts. Both daughters work coöperatively with their mother—cooking, grinding corn, and the like. The old couple frequently slaughter a sheep and occasionally a calf or cow, and portion the meat to their daughters on their frequent visits.

Paul, the old man, owns a wagon and a team of horses. The team and wagon are used by the sons-in-law whenever they have need of them. Recently Josie and John bought a pickup truck, and the vehicle has to a large extent displaced the wagon and team. Since Josie is regularly employed at Keams Canyon, she made the initial down payment on the truck, I was told, and John and Peter helped her on the monthly payments. Paul drives a car, and until he became blind about a year ago he used the truck as much as John. At the present time the old couple ask one of their sons-in-law to drive for them whenever they wish to go anywhere. Peter uses the truck for transporting his immediate family or for performing services for the benefit of the extended household. I was told that the person using the car at a given time is supposed to pay for gas and oil and for light repairs; for major repairs a contribution is taken from all adult members of the household. Hopi and Hopi-Tewa give their cars rough treatment. The farms and ranches to which they travel most frequently are situated in remote areas, and the roads are extremely bad. During the initial phases of my study when I lived in one of the Hopi-Tewa households, my 1949 Jeep Station Wagon became household property, and since none of the members could drive, I was the chauffeur. I hauled sheep, calves, and wood in my car and transported members of the household to various parts of the reservation, and on several occasions to the off-reservation towns of Gallup, Holbrook, and Winslow. Although the members of the household were generous in providing gas and oil, I was glad that the following year I could live below the mesa and be relieved of the responsibility.

Major interaction, sharing, and coöperation goes on within the household unit. In social and ceremonial functions embracing larger units, the activity is initiated within the household but is intricately fitted into the larger coöperating units, whether clan, kiva group, community, or intervillage.

SHARING WITHIN THE CLAN AND PHRATRY

The clan and its linked clans[11] function as economic coöperative units in many social and ceremonial functions. For an illustration of the activities in such an interacting unit, a wedding has been selected. A wedding is primarily a social event, but like all other activities of the Hopi and Hopi-Tewa it also has ceremonial features.

The wedding to be discussed is one between a Hopi-Tewa Cottonwood girl and a Hopi Butterfly boy, which took place in January, 1950. The boy had been secretly courting the girl and presumably had been having sexual relations with her. (The boys sneak out together, and each meets his sweetheart at a secret rendezvous or at

---

[11] That is, clans exogamically linked. See section on "The Clan," in chap. iii, for a list of clans and a discussion of linked clans.

her house after her family are asleep.) Sanction of the marriage was obtained when the girl took up residence with the boy's family at Sichomovi and was permitted to stay.[12] Immediately she began to grind corn in a darkened corn-grinding room. Theoretically, she was supposed to grind corn for three days and four nights by herself, but actually all her clanswomen assisted. Not only did the women of her own Cottonwood clan help, but also those of the Hopi Kachina clan, which the Hopi consider related to that clan. These women ground corn in their own homes and brought it to her and also assisted her in the darkened room, in which she remained the traditional four-day and four-night period.

In the meantime, all the men of the girl's clan and linked clans brought food to the bridegroom's house; during this four-day period they slaughtered sheep and cattle, brought firewood, and helped the women carry the food. A special room, about fifteen by twenty feet, was set aside to hold the food gifts. At the end of the four days the room was entirely filled with food: basins of stew, roasted meats, stewed peaches, yellow corn-meal cakes, sugar-frosted baked cakes, pies, and other foods covered the entire floor space; sacks of wheat flour were piled almost to the ceiling against one wall; on the opposite side, piki was stacked like cordwood halfway up to the ceiling. On the last day, when most of the food was brought in, five pickup trucks drove into the plaza in front of the bridegroom's house and unloaded enormous trays of corn meal. Each truck contained about a dozen trays, approximately fifteen to twenty inches in diameter, heaped with tightly compacted corn meal to a height of two feet or more. Large flour-sack cloths were tied about the trays to protect the corn meal. Some trays were so heavy that it required three or more men to lift and carry them.

The food brought by the girl's family was shared by the clansfolk of the bridegroom and also by those of the linked Badger clan. On the evening of the fourth day all the women of these clans visited the boy's house and were given large quantities of food to take home with them, each woman receiving an approximately equal amount.

SHARING WITHIN A KIVA GROUP

In certain social and ceremonial functions the unit of coöperative activity is the kiva group, that is, the clans belonging to one of the two Hopi-Tewa kivas. These functions occur with less frequency than clan-phratry functions but are similar coöperative affairs, differing only in that more people take part in them. The activities that characterize kiva group enterprises will be illustrated by a discussion of a social dance.

On June 24, 1950, a *Yandewa* Dance was given by members of the Central Plaza Kiva at Tewa Village. For a whole month previously, however, preparations and rehearsals had been under way. The *Yandewa* is a colorful dance originally borrowed from Santa Clara Pueblo.[13] For this occasion I made a trip to Santa Clara and brought back with me three Tewa men. As honored guests we were permitted to watch all the preparations for the dance inside the kiva.

Twice during the day of the dance, first at midday and again in late afternoon,

---

[12] After presenting corn meal to her prospective mother-in-law. For a more detailed account of wedding customs see above, pp. 329–330.

[13] There are four dancers in each of eight plaza appearances—two young men and two girls—thirty-two dancers in all. All the men belonging to the clans of the kiva join in the chorus and help in many other ways inside the kiva.

all the adult women of the clans that belong to the Central Plaza Kiva—Bear, Corn, Tobacco, Fir—brought in enormous quantities of food. On each occasion the kiva chief distributed the food equally among all those present in the kiva. My share was two washtubs of bread, crackers, candy, piki bread, and various other foods. In addition, there were large quantities of prepared foods in bowls and pans, such as stews, roasted meats, jerky (sun-dried strips of beef), cornmeal gruel, and the like. The prepared foods were also divided, as equally as possible, among the men. After each "giving" the men carried their portions of the food to their respective homes. I presented my share to my hosts at Tewa Village.

COMMUNITY SHARING

Although in a wedding only two clans and their linked clans are involved, other ceremonial and social activities bring together the whole community. In all such activities, however, the pattern of exchange of food and services operates within the clan unit or the group of clans belonging to each kiva. Coöperative enterprises which are essentially communal include hunting, planting, harvesting, cleaning springs, and gathering firewood for the kivas. Such enterprises are initiated by one of the men; they are announced by the War Chief and are participated in by all able-bodied men, while the women grind corn and cook to feed the whole community. After such an enterprise the men gather in the kiva to offer thanksgiving or to put on a social dance, and the food is given and shared, as described above, for the Yandewa. Each man, with his share of food, then returns to his own household.

The following account of the general requirements and procedure of a working party[14] was related to me by one of my Hopi-Tewa informants:

> Whenever a man decides to have a working party he asks permission from the Village Chief. The petition is made by presenting the chief with a basket or bowl of corn meal. If the chief accepts the meal the petitioner starts preparations right away. He makes several prayer feathers and abstains from meat and salt for four days. During this time he must not sleep with his wife. At the end of four days he asks the War Chief to announce the working party to the whole village. The petitioner then supervises the work, but he is assisted by all of his clanspeople and his paternal aunts [i.e., women of his father's clan]. All those men who are not actively engaged in the work are put to other tasks. Some of the men must go for firewood, others for water and cattle. Women and girls must grind corn and prepare food to feed not only the men actively engaged in the working party but the entire village. Everyone helps to make the working party a success. While working all the people are happy; jokes and stories are told so that work becomes like play. Later there is a dance given by the kiva groups, and everyone goes home loaded with food.

INTERVILLAGE SHARING

First Mesa Hopi ceremonies of major importance, such as the Tribal Initiation which occurs in certain years in November, the Niman in July, and the Snake Dance in August, are occasions in which all three villages coöperate. Only a few Hopi-Tewa are active participants in Hopi ceremonies, but marriage ties with the Hopi relate them to participants in these ceremonies. Tewa women are thus as active as Hopi women in preparing and buying food to be taken to the men who are participating in the ceremonies. Hopi-Tewa men are busy butchering, hauling wood, and making food supplies available for the women. Teams and wagons and, more re-

---

[14] Parsons' journalist, a Hopi-Tewa man, relates an interesting account of a working party for the Village Chief in 1921 (see Parsons, 1925, pp. 112–115).

cently, automobiles are put to use to assist in the transportation of foodstuffs. The contributed food is taken to the Walpi kivas in which these ceremonies take place; division and disposal of the food operates in the manner described for kiva group ceremonials above. The day of the dance is given over to elaborate feasting—every home setting out food for guests from other Hopi villages and for Indian visitors from other tribes. In recent years, special white friends have also been honored as guests. The festive spirit and coöperative activity of the people of First Mesa in a major ceremonial is an interesting and impressive sight.

TRADING PARTIES

Another interesting coöperative activity of First Mesa villages is the trading party. This activity is initiated by a household and is open to anyone in the three villages; indeed, visitors, Indian or white, may participate. My wife was a frequent "trader" during our residence at Polacca. Trading parties occur with great frequency— "about two or three times a month," my hostess reported.

Most of the participants are women, though men are not barred. Men are supposed to contribute game, and when I appeared for the first time at a trading party the women greeted me in a chorus: "Where is your deer meat, where are your rabbits?" But they took the cigarettes, soft drinks, and wheat flour I brought, and I received in return "hot tamales," piki, and doughnuts.

The trading party is held outdoors, in front of the house of the family that initiates it. The food, clothing, and other articles brought by those participating are spread out on the ground, while the "traders" stand around in a circle. The articles brought to be traded are extremely varied. I have seen chinaware, shoes, overalls, and toys (bought in town), along with the more common items, such as Hopi pottery and baskets, piki, oven-baked bread, meat stews, cakes, pies, and wheat and corn flour.

There is very little bargaining at a trading party. Hopi and Hopi-Tewa trade in a friendly, noncompetetive fashion. A "trader" walks to the article that catches his fancy, finds out who the owner is, and then trading is conducted between the two people. The food or goods traded are generally those displayed; but if a person who wishes an article does not have an item at hand which the owner wants in exchange, she may mention a number of articles at home which she is willing to give for the desired article. Exchanges are made in the most agreeable and friendly manner. I saw no attempts "to drive a hard bargain." The people seem to have no notion of getting more for an item, or one of a better quality, in exchange. When I asked my hostess why the trading parties were so popular she replied:

"Because we have a good time, we joke, laugh, and tease each other when we trade. In the evening we return home with a variety of things. Some people don't have meat, others have no flour, or piki, or cigarettes—we trade and everybody gets the things they want."

SUMMARY

From the discussion of economic activities, we can conclude that although horticulture is still basic in Hopi-Tewa economy, wage work and livestock have come to form a very important part of their economic system. At present the social organization of the Hopi-Tewa is still operating chiefly in terms of the traditional patterns of the extended-household and clan structures. A number of factors have brought about this situation. First, livestock and wage-work activities, particularly the latter, are recent innovations. Secondly, modern transportation facilities have made possible frequent resumptions of extended-household living and interaction in terms of clans and groups of clans. Thirdly, the satisfaction derived from the extended household and clan and the rich ceremonial life of community living have not been matched elsewhere.

The coöperative enterprises characteristic of social and ceremonial functions have prevented pronounced differences in the economic standing of Hopi-Tewa families and generally of the families in all three communities on First Mesa. These customs are remarkably strong and complex and indicate continuity in the future, despite modern pressures. The coöperation of Hopi-Tewa and Hopi in these functions points to greater cohesion in the future, thus minimizing social barriers between the two groups and working toward a coalescence of First Mesa society.

CHAPTER VI

SUMMARY AND CONCLUSIONS

THE SOCIAL, ceremonial, and economic organization of the Hopi-Tewa has been discussed in detail in the preceding chapters. The study may now be summarized. It is also important to restate the changes brought about by white contact and to discuss the present position of the Hopi-Tewa as an integral part of First Mesa society as a whole.

To isolate aspects of Hopi-Tewa culture which appear to be unique to the group is difficult since affinities to both Rio Grande Tewa and Hopi appear in all areas. There is one respect, however, in which the Hopi-Tewa seem to differ from both Hopi and Rio Grande Tewa; this is in the realm of personality. The Hopi-Tewa appear to be more aggressive, and more willing to accept white ways and to coöperate with the local Indian Service. The individual Hopi-Tewa is friendly to whites and has little of the reticence characteristic of both the Hopi and the Rio Grande Tewa.

It is not known what factors are responsible for creating a personality structure among the Hopi-Tewa that is at variance with that of other pueblo peoples. Certain hypotheses may be ventured, however. First, the Hopi-Tewa were formerly on the eastern frontier of the pueblo area, and there they interacted with Plains Indian tribes. Second, they had a history of resistance to the Spaniards but escaped to Hopi before becoming completely subdued. Third, their minority status at Hopi may well have demanded the assertion of personality traits antithetical to the Hopi. At Hopi the aggressive, independent traits of the Hopi-Tewa were encouraged by their position as warriors and protectors of the Hopi.

Any one or all of these factors may account for the formation of Hopi-Tewa personality. The fact is that, at present, Hopi-Tewa attitudes and behavior contrast sharply with the Hopi.

In spite of the Hopi-Tewa's friendly and coöperative relations with whites, these Indians have not become pronouncedly acculturated to American life. Hopi-Tewa culture appears to be well integrated along traditional lines. Certain important changes have come about, however, as the result of modern pressures. The most important are the periodic reductions of the matrilineal extended household to meet demands imposed by livestock and wage-work activities. As a result of modern conditions, too, a few of the young people, particularly those who have gone to schools outside the reservation, are encountering problems of adjustment. The older people make much of this, yet these deviations from the norm may express no more than the behavior characteristic of the younger generation in any society.

Although it is possible to see both Hopi and Rio Grande Tewa elements in Hopi-Tewa social and ceremonial organization, these have been so thoroughly integrated into Hopi-Tewa culture that the group differs significantly from the other two. As might be expected from the long residence of the Hopi-Tewa on First Mesa, their culture more closely resembles that of the Hopi. Thus, Hopi-Tewa social and ceremonial organization is founded on the same principles as the Hopi: the kinship system, household, clan, ceremonial societies, and kiva groups. But in all these institutions certain similarities to the Rio Grande Tewa appear—areas in which they differ from the Hopi.

The greatest difference between Hopi-Tewa and Hopi culture is in ceremonial organization. The dual or moiety concept is here emphasized, not only in migration legends and myths but in actual structural make-up. The two kiva groups at Tewa Village function independently of each other in the performance of various ceremonials. There is a leader, or chief, for each group, as among the Rio Grande Tewa. The Hopi-Tewa hold kiva group initiations which are suggestive of Tewa moiety initiations in New Mexico. Until recently, Tewa Village had a katcina cult, essentially different from that of the Hopi but closely resembling the Rio Grande Tewa katcina organization. In the emphasis on curing in their ceremonies, the Hopi-Tewa again contrast with the Hopi and indicate retention of Rio Grande ceremonial concepts.

Hopi-Tewa social and ceremonial organization thus appears to be the result of (1) a core of elements indigenous to the group and bearing resemblances to the Rio Grande Tewa, (2) elements borrowed from the Hopi over a period of two and a half centuries during which the two groups have lived as neighbors, and (3) a unique integration of the two that appears to be becoming progressively a new whole.

Hopi-Tewa economy is still to a large extent dependent on farming, handicrafts, and other traditional occupations, although wage work and livestock raising have become extremely important in recent years. The economy is still functioning mainly in terms of the traditional patterns of the extended-household and clan structures. A number of factors have helped make these patterns important. First, livestock and wage-work activities, particularly the latter, are recent innovations. Second, modern transportation facilities have made possible frequent resumptions of extended-household living and interaction in terms of clans and groups of clans. Third, the satisfactions derived from the extended household, clan, and the rich ceremonial life of community living have not been matched elsewhere.

Potential threats to the household and clan structures are, however, clear. The Hopi-Tewa's increasing relations with whites are drawing them more and more into the American pecuniary economic system. It is possible that as succeeding generations grow up, away from the close touch of the extended household and clan relatives, the importance of the nuclear family will increase. New generations may find satisfactions within a new pattern of relationships and value systems. On the other hand, native customs are strong and complex and apparently will long continue despite modern pressures. The Hopi and Hopi-Tewa have thus far adjusted to modern pressures, and there is no reason why they cannot continue to make such adjustments while preserving most of their own traditional social and ceremonial organization.

THE HOPI-TEWA AS PART OF FIRST MESA SOCIETY

The most significant aspect of the present study is the trend toward social integration[1] of the three communities on First Mesa. The Hopi-Tewa appear to have become accepted by the Hopi as "equals," and social organizational differences are becoming minimized. The change in conditions has taken place so recently that many Hopi and Hopi-Tewa inhabitants remember the former period of animosity

[1] "Social integration" instead of "cultural integration" is used advisedly. The people of the three communities on First Mesa are closely interrelated in a network of interpersonal relationships for the purpose of achieving a harmonious life (social integration); but their belief systems, attitudes, and behavior patterns (cultural phenomena) are not necessarily integrated. For a clear distinction between social and cultural integration, see Eggan, 1950, pp. 6 ff.

between the two peoples. The change in attitudes began about sixty or seventy years ago when Anglo-Americans began to come in increasing numbers. The phenomenon appears directly related to this early white contact. The situation seems to be that Anglo-Americans brought Hopi-Tewa and Hopi together through a change in value orientation. Until the Americans came, the value system of the Hopi-Tewa occupied a "back seat" in Hopi culture. Hopi-Tewa value orientation is at variance with that of the Hopi, but it is remarkably like that of Anglo-American culture. It is not surprising, then, that the Hopi-Tewa "got along" with the early whites. When the situation changed and they came to believe that "it paid to be like the whites," the Hopi began to regard the Hopi-Tewa more favorably. Gradually compromises were made—ceremonially the Hopi-Tewa deferred to the Hopi, and the Hopi accommodated to the Hopi-Tewa in secular affairs.

In terms of social integration, First Mesa villages contrast sharply with other Hopi village groups. Hopi authorities characterize Hopi society as poorly integrated. Titiev (1944, p. 69), for example, reports:

... [The Hopi] social system rests on unstable foundations, for the more firmly people adhere to clan lines, the weaker must be their village ties. A Hopi pueblo is like an object with a thin outer shell which holds together a number of firm distinct segments [the clans]; should the shell be cracked the segments would fall apart ... That such breakdowns have frequently taken place in the past can be readily established by the archaeological record in the Southwest which seems to indicate that "long before the advent of the Conquistadores the habit of town splitting must have developed. ...

Titiev (1944, p. 68) ends a chapter on Hopi political organization with the following statement:

... Within each village the lack of a strong central authority permits the growth of factions and leads to schisms; and between pueblo and pueblo there is an attitude of jealousy, suspicion, and subdued hostility. Never has any town been entirely free from strife, and never has a leader arisen to mould the autonomous villages into a coordinated unit worthy of being a tribe. Whatever other talents they may possess, the Hopi do not have the gift of statecraft. ...

Eggan (1950, pp. 118–119) concurs with Titiev. In describing Hopi village integration, he reports:

A strong clan system, other things being equal, is correlated with a weak political system ... Hopi ideology forbids the use of force, and quarrels are antithetical to village welfare. The achievement of unanimity by consensus is the desired end but becomes increasingly difficult to attain.

... All villages are beset with factions which argue endlessly and disrupt the smooth operation of village life. No village has achieved a solution of the factional problem, and, where the factions become strong enough, they bring about further splitting.

In contrast to other major Hopi village groups, the three communities on First Mesa have attained a comparatively high degree of integration in recent years. The test findings of the Indian Personality and Administration Research directed by Dr. Laura Thompson have revealed this situation (see Thompson and Joseph, 1944; Thompson, 1950). Thompson attributes the integration to a retention of traditional Hopi social organization. She points out that disintegrative processes have set in only at Third Mesa since there have been land restrictions and adverse white contacts, particularly missionary activities, which have disturbed the original socioreligious organization. She reports (1950, p. 77):

The structural imbalance which characterizes the Oraibi socioreligious system as compared to that of First Mesa is reflected in test findings of the present project. The findings indicate that at Oraibi the nicely adjusted, dynamic balance of the traditional Hopi social organization . . . has been thrown "out of kilter."

About the situation on First Mesa, she remarks (1950, pp. 79–80): .

Turning to the present research findings from First Mesa, where the ceremonial cycle is still relatively intact, we see a much more balanced social set-up revealed by the tests. This appears not only in the family, where both the mother and the father have an important place, but also between the family and the community. Whereas in Oraibi most of the child's sanctions come directly from the tightly bound but shrinking kinship group with the mother at its head, at First Mesa they are less direct and more diffuse. At First Mesa the family, the community, and the supernatural world reinforce one another in both a positive and a negative role.

Moreover, at First Mesa intense ceremonial activity and less pronounced economic pressures seem to be clearly reflected in several ways: (1) in the responsiveness and spontaneity of the First Mesa boys; (2) in the healthy "social climate"; (3) in the presence of active, successful cattle cooperatives; and (4) in the unification of all villages of the mesa into one political unit which functions under the leadership of the traditional pueblo chiefs.

My findings tend to corroborate the results obtained by the Indian Personality and Administration Research team at First Mesa. The integration is not as thorough as that described by Thompson; it is only so when compared with other groups of Hopi villages. My interpretation of the causes of relative integration on First Mesa is also at variance with that of Thompson. Social integration on First Mesa is quite recent and is actually on the increase, and it is not due to traditional Hopi social organization. Indeed, the studies of Titiev and Eggan indicate that if the villages were united solely on traditional Hopi patterns of social organization, a weaker organization would have resulted. My data suggest that the Hopi-Tewa had a major role in bringing about unity of the three villages on First Mesa. Thus, social integration was effected by a foreign group and not by the Hopi alone.

The Hopi research team directed by Thompson excluded the Hopi-Tewa from the tests apparently because inclusion might have invalidated the conclusions of a study designed to measure the Hopi specifically. The wisdom of this action may be questioned. The Hopi-Tewa are an integral part of the Hopi of First Mesa; they are so interrelated through marriage and in other diverse ways that it would be very difficult to separate them from their neighbors. Although the influences of white contacts, especially of missionaries, were considered in detail by Thompson, a group consisting of more than one-third of the population of First Mesa and in constant contact with the Hopi for more than 250 years was utterly disregarded. In actuality, of course, the influence of the Hopi-Tewa figured into the findings in spite of precautions to the contrary.

I have not attempted a detailed analysis of Hopi-Tewa influences on Hopi, though such influences appear to be considerable. Some authorities have categorized the traits diffused to the Hopi from the Hopi-Tewa. Among these are the curing emphasis in ceremonies, clown groups (Koshare), ritual shinny, the Hopi Butterfly Dance, and the Hopi Buffalo Dance.[2] Undoubtedly, personality traits have also diffused, particularly in recent years with increasing intermarriages. It is to be expected that the Hopi of First Mesa would be most influenced by Hopi-Tewa. The

---

[2] See Eggan, 1950, pp. 172–173; Parsons, 1939, pp. 970–971.

Hopi from other villages and white Indian Service workers distinguish the Tewa from the Hopi, and usually First Mesa Hopi from other Hopi, on the basis of behavior. The Hopi of other villages regard First Mesa inhabitants as "mostly Tewa" and as characterized by erratic behavior of the kind attributed to the Hopi-Tewa. A Shongopovi resident, while giving me his opinion of the Panchale dance recently introduced by the Rio Grande Tewa, also revealed his estimation of First Mesa Hopi:

"Oh, those First Mesa people, they are crazy like the Tewa. They will do anything. They put on these crazy Panchale dances which are a disgrace to the Hopi. It used to be that only Tewa did that dance, but now all the First Mesa Hopi also do it. Maybe they are even worse than the Tewa; they always do things together, anyway."

The part played by the Hopi-Tewa in bringing about greater integration on First Mesa can be summarized briefly: The advent of Anglo-Americans brought about a value orientation that approximated that of the Hopi-Tewa. The traits of the Hopi-Tewa that formerly seemed objectionable to the Hopi—aggressiveness, friendliness to outsiders, willingness to coöperate with Americans, eagerness to adopt white techniques and economic pursuits, and the like—began to have definite status value. Gradually some of these traits were also adopted by First Mesa Hopi, and eventually their goals became unified.

A second major factor leading to integration has to do with the assumption of secular roles of responsibility traditionally avoided by the Hopi. These are the positions of interpreter, policeman, and other contact positions with outsiders which in recent years have been filled primarily by Hopi-Tewa.

The result of the integration has been the acceleration of borrowing between the two groups. First Mesa now has a unity and an integration which it lacked in the past. There is still a distinction between the two groups, but the difference is complementary. Thus, the Hopi-Tewa have deferred to the Hopi ceremonially while they have gained in secular and social participation.

BIBLIOGRAPHY

(Only references cited in text)

BAILEY, J. B.
    1940. *Diego de Vargas and the Reconquest of New Mexico.* University of New Mexico Press, Albuquerque.
BAILEY, PAUL
    1948. *Jacob Hamblin, Buckskin Apostle.* Western Lore Press, Los Angeles.
BANCROFT, H. H.
    1888. *History of Arizona and New Mexico.* San Francisco.
BANDELIER, A. F.
    1890–1892. *Final Report of Investigations among the Indians of the Southwestern United States.* Papers of the Archaeological Institute of America: American Series, Vol. III, Pt. 1, and Vol. IV, Pt. 2. Cambridge, Mass.
BARTLETT, KATHERINE
    1934. "Spanish Contacts with the Hopi, 1540–1823," *Museum Notes*, Vol. VI, No. 12, pp. 55–60. Northern Arizona Society of Science and Art, Flagstaff.
    1936. "Hopi History, No. II: The Navaho Wars, 1823–1870," *Museum Notes*, Vol. VIII, No. 7, pp. 33–37. Northern Arizona Society of Science and Art, Flagstaff.
BEADLE, J. H.
    ⌐ 1878. *Western Wilds, and the Men Who Redeem Them; an Authentic Narrative.* Cincinnati.
BEAGLEHOLE, ERNEST
    1937. *Notes on Hopi Economic Life.* Yale University Publications in Anthropology, No. 15. New Haven, Conn.
BLOOM, L. B.
    1931. "A Campaign against the Moqui Pueblos," *New Mexico Historical Review*, Vol. VI, No. 2, pp. 158–226.
    1935. "Albuquerque and Galisteo, Certificate of Their Founding, 1706," *New Mexico Historical Review*, Vol. X, No. 2, pp. 48–50.
BOLTON, H. E.
    1916. "The Espejo Expedition, 1582–1583," *in* H. E. Bolton, *Spanish Exploration in the Southwest, 1542–1706*, pp. 161–196. Charles Scribner's Sons, New York.
BRADLEY, G. D.
    1920. *The Story of the Santa Fe.* Richard G. Badger, Boston.
BRYAN, K.
    1929. "Flood-water Farming," *Geographical Review*, Vol. 19, No. 3, pp. 444–456.
COLTON, H. S.
    1930. "A Brief Survey of the Early Expeditions into Northern Arizona," *Museum Notes*, Vol. II, No. 9, pp. 1–4. Northern Arizona Society of Science and Art, Flagstaff.
COZZENS, S. W.
    1873. *The Marvellous Country; or, Three Years in Arizona and New Mexico, the Apaches' Home.* Boston.
CRANE, LEO
    1925. *Indians of the Painted Desert.* Little, Brown, Boston.
CUSHING, F. H., J. W. FEWKES, AND E. C. PARSONS
    1922. "Contributions to Hopi History," *American Anthropologist*, n.s., Vol. 24, No. 3, pp. 253–298.
DOUGLAS, A. E.
    1935. "Estimated Ring Chronology II: 1650–1800," *Tree Ring Bulletin*, Vol. 1, No. 4, pp. 27–29.
DOZIER, E. P.
    1951. "Resistance to Acculturation and Assimilation in an Indian Pueblo," *American Anthropologist*, n.s., Vol. 53, No. 1, pp. 56–65.
    MS. "The Changing Social Organization of the Hopi-Tewa." Unpublished Ph.D. dissertation, University of California, Los Angeles, 1952.

EGGAN, FRED
1937. "The Cheyenne and Arapaho Kinship System," *in* Eggan (ed.), *Social Anthropology of North American Tribes*, pp. 33–95. University of Chicago Press.
1950. *Social Organization of the Western Pueblos*. University of Chicago Press.

ELLIS, FLORENCE HAWLEY
1951. "Pueblo Social Organization and Southwestern Archaeology," *American Antiquity*, Vol. 17, pp. 148–151.

ESPINOSA, GILBERTO
1933. *History of New Mexico, by Gaspar Pérez de Villagrá, Alcalá, 1610*. Translated by Gilberto Espinosa; introduction and notes by F. W. Hodge. The Quivira Society, Los Angeles.

ESPINOSA, J. M.
1940. *First Expedition of Vargas into New Mexico, 1692*. Translated, with introduction and notes by J. Manuel Espinosa. Coronado Historical Series, Vol. X. University of New Mexico Press, Albuquerque.

FEWKES, J. W.
1894. "The Kinship of a Tanoan Speaking Community in Tusayan," *American Anthropologist*, o.s., Vol. 7, No. 2, pp. 162–167.
1899. "The Winter Solstice Altars of Hano Pueblo," *American Anthropologist*, n.s., Vol. 1, No. 2, pp. 251–276.
1902. "Tusayan Migration Traditions," *Nineteenth Annual Report [for 1900]*, Pt. 2, Bureau of American Ethnology, pp. 577–633. Smithsonian Institution, Washington.
1922. "Ancestor Worship of the Hopi Indians," *Annual Report of the . . . Smithsonian Institution for the Year Ending June 30, 1921*, pp. 485–506. Washington.

FORDE, C. D.
1931. "Hopi Agriculture and Land Ownership," *Journal of the Royal Anthropological Institute*, Vol. 61, pp. 357–411.

FREIRE-MARRECO, BARBARA
1914. "Tewa Kinship Terms from the Pueblo of Hano, Arizona," *American Anthropologist*, n.s., Vol. 16, No. 2, pp. 269–287.

GILLIN, JOHN
1948. *The Ways of Man*. Appleton-Century, New York.

GOLDFRANK, E. S.
1927. *The Social and Ceremonial Organization of Cochiti*. Memoirs of the American Anthropological Association, No. 33. Menasha, Wis.

HACK, J. T.
1942. *The Changing Physical Environment of the Hopi Indians of Arizona*. Peabody Museum of American Archaeology and Ethnology, Papers, Vol. 35, No. 1. Cambridge, Mass.

HACKETT, C. W., AND C. C. SHELBY
1942. *Revolt of the Pueblo Indians of New Mexico and Otermin's Attempted Reconquest, 1680–1682*. Coronado Historical Series, Vols. VIII and IX. University of New Mexico Press, Albuquerque.

HAMMOND, G. P.
1926. "Don Juan de Oñate, and the Founding of New Mexico," *New Mexico Historical Review*, Vol. I, No. 1, pp. 42–77; No. 2, pp. 156–192.

HAMMOND, G. P., AND AGAPITO REY
1927. *The Gallegos Relation of the Rodriguez Expedition to New Mexico*. Translated and edited by G. P. Hammond and Agapito Rey. Historical Society of New Mexico, Publications in History, Vol. IV. Santa Fe.
1929. *Expedition into New Mexico Made by Antonio de Espejo, 1582–1583, as Revealed in the Journal of Diego Pérez de Luxán, a Member of the Party*. Translated, with introduction and notes by G. P. Hammond and Agapito Rey.

HARRINGTON, J. P.
1912. "Tewa Relationship Terms," *American Anthropologist*, n.s., Vol. 14, No. 3, pp. 472–498.

HAWLEY, FLORENCE
1937. "Pueblo Social Organization as a Lead to Pueblo History," *American Anthropologist*, n.s., Vol. 39, No. 3, Pt. 1, pp. 504–522.

HAWLEY, FLORENCE (*Continued*)

1950a. "Big Kivas, Little Kivas and Moiety Houses in Historical Reconstruction," *Southwestern Journal of Anthropology*, Vol. 6, No. 3, pp. 286–302.

1950b. "Keresan Patterns of Kinship and Social Organization," *American Anthropologist*, n.s., Vol. 52, No. 4, Pt. 1, pp. 499–512.

HILL, W. W.

1936. *Navaho Warfare.* Yale University Publications in Anthropology, No. 5. Yale University Press, New Haven, Conn.

MS.   Santa Clara Pueblo. In the possession of its author, Department of Anthropology, University of New Mexico, Albuquerque.

HODGE, F. W.

1896. "Pueblo Indian Clans," *American Anthropologist*, o.s., Vol. 9, No. 10, pp. 345–352.

1907. "The Narrative of the Expedition of Coronado, by Pedro de Castañeda," *in* F. W. Hodge and T. H. Lewis (eds.), *Spanish Explorers in the Southern United States, 1528–1543*, pp. 275–387. Charles Scribner's Sons, New York.

1912. (ed.) *Handbook of American Indians North of Mexico.* Bull. 30, Pts. 1 and 2. Bureau of American Ethnology, Smithsonian Institution, Washington.

HODGE, F. W., G. P. HAMMOND, AND AGAPITO REY

1945. *Revised Memorial of Alonzo de Benavides, 1634.* Coronado Historical Series, Vol. IV. University of New Mexico Press, Albuquerque.

HOIJER, HARRY

1946. "Introduction," *in* Harry Hoijer and others, *Linguistic Structures of Native America*, pp. 9–29. Viking Fund Publications in Anthropology, No. 6. New York.

HOIJER, HARRY, AND E. P. DOZIER

1949. "The Phonemes of Tewa, Santa Clara Dialect," *International Journal of American Linguistics*, Vol. 15, No. 3, pp. 139–144.

JONES, V. H.

1950. "The Establishment of the Hopi Reservation and Some Later Developments Concerning Hopi Lands," *Plateau*, Vol. 23, No. 2, pp. 17–25. Northern Arizona Society of Science and Art, Flagstaff.

LA FARGE, OLIVER

MS.   Personal notes on the organization of the Hopi tribe, 1936.

LOWIE, R. H.

1929. *Notes on Hopi Clans.* Anthropological Papers of the American Museum of Natural History, Vol. 30, Pt. 6. New York.

MINDELEFF, VICTOR

1891. "A Study of Pueblo Architecture," *Eighth Annual Report [for 1886–1887]*, Bureau of American Ethnology, pp. 1–288. Smithsonian Institution, Washington.

MONTGOMERY, R. G., WATSON SMITH, AND J. O. BREW

1949. *Franciscan Awatovi.* Peabody Museum of American Archaeology and Ethnology, Papers, Vol. 36. Cambridge, Mass.

MURDOCK, G. P.

1949. *Social Structure.* Macmillan, New York.

NARVÁEZ VALVERDE, FRAY JOSÉ

1937. "Notes upon Moqui and Other Recent Ones upon New Mexico," *in* C. W. Hackett (ed.), *Historical Documents Relating to New Mexico, Vizcaya, and Approaches Thereto, to 1773.* Vol. III, pp. 385–387. Carnegie Institution of Washington.

NELSON, N. C.

1914. *Pueblo Ruins of the Galisteo Basin, New Mexico.* Anthropological Papers of the American Museum of Natural History, Vol. 15, Pt. 1. New York.

NEQUATEWA, EDMUND

1936. *Truth of a Hopi and Other Clan Stories of Shung-opovi.* Ed. by Mary-Russell F. Colton. Museum of Northern Arizona, Bull. No. 8. Northern Arizona Society of Science and Art, Flagstaff.

PARSONS, E. C.

1921a. "Hopi Mothers and Children," *Man*, Vol. 21, No. 58, pp. 98–104.

1921b. "Getting Married on First Mesa, Arizona," *Scientific Monthly*, Vol. 13, No. 3, pp. 209–216.

1923. "The Hopi Buffalo Dance," *Man*, Vol. 23, No. 12, pp. 21–26.

1925. *A Pueblo Indian Journal, 1920–21*, Memoirs of the American Anthropological Association, No. 32. Menasha, Wis.

1926. "The Ceremonial Calendar of the Tewa of Arizona," *American Anthropologist*, n.s., Vol. 28, No. 1, pp. 209–229.

1927. "Witchcraft among the Pueblos: Indian or Spanish?" *Man*, Vol. 27, No. 70, pp. 106–112; No. 80, pp. 125–128.

1929. *The Social Organization of the Tewa of New Mexico*. Memoirs of the American Anthropological Association, No. 36. Menasha, Wis.

1936a. "Introduction" *in* E. C. Parsons (ed.), *Hopi Journal*. Columbia University, Contributions to Anthropology, Vol. 23, Pt. 1, pp. xxv–lii.

1936b. *Taos Pueblo*. General Series in Anthropology, No. 2. Menasha, Wis.

1939. Pueblo Indian Religion. 2 vols. University of Chicago Press.

PRINCE, L. B.
1912. *A Concise History of New Mexico*. The Torch Press, Cedar Rapids, Ia.

REED, ERIK
1942. "Kawaik-a in the Historic Period," *American Anthropologist*, n.s., Vol. 8, No. 1, pp. 119–120.

1943a. "The Origins of Hano Pueblo," *El Palacio*, Vol. 50, No. 4, pp. 73–76.

1943b. "The Southern Tewa Pueblos in the Historic Period," *El Palacio*, Vol. 50, No. 11, pp. 254–264; No. 12, pp. 276–288.

1950. "Eastern-Central Arizona Archaeology in Relation to the Western Pueblos," *Southwestern Journal of Anthropology*, Vol. 6, No. 2, pp. 120–138.

1952. "The Tewa Indians of the Hopi Country," *Plateau*, Vol. 25, No. 1, pp. 11–18.

SCHOLES, F. V.
1935. "The First Decade of the Inquisition in New Mexico," *New Mexico Historical Review*, Vol. 10, No. 3, pp. 195–241.

1936–1937. "Church and State in New Mexico," *New Mexico Historical Review*, Vol. 11, No. 1, pp. 9–76; No. 2, pp. 145–178; No. 3, pp. 283–294; No. 4, pp. 297–349; Vol. 12, No. 1, pp. 78–106.

1942. *Troublous Times in New Mexico, 1659–1670*. Historical Society of New Mexico, Publications in History, Vol. 11. Albuquerque.

SCHOLES, F. V., AND L. B. BLOOM
1944–1945. "Friar Personnel and Mission Chronology, 1598–1629," *New Mexico Historical Review*, Vol. 19, No. 4, pp. 319–336; Vol. 20, No. 1, pp. 58–82.

SPIER, LESLIE
1925. "The Distribution of Kinship Systems in North America," *University of Washington Publications in Anthropology*, Vol. 1, No. 2, pp. 71–88.

STEPHEN, A. M.
1936. *Hopi Journal*. Edited by E. C. Parsons. Columbia University, Contributions to Anthropology, Vol. 23, Pts. 1 and 2.

STEVENSON, M. C.
1894. "The Sia," *Eleventh Annual Report [for 1889–1890]*, Bureau of American Ethnology, pp. 3–157. Smithsonian Institution, Washington.

STEWART, G. R.
1940. "Conservation in Pueblo Agriculture," *Scientific Monthly*, Vol. 51, No. 4, pp. 201–220.

THOMAS, A. B.
1932. *Forgotten Frontiers, a Study of the Spanish Indian Policy of Don Juan Bautista de Anza, Governor of New Mexico, 1777–1787*. University of Oklahoma Press, Norman.

THOMPSON, LAURA
1950. *Culture in Crisis, a Study of the Hopi Indians*. Harper, New York.

THOMPSON, LAURA, AND ALICE JOSEPH
1944. *The Hopi Way*. United States Indian Service, Lawrence, Kan.

TITIEV, MISCHA
1944. *Old Oraibi, a Study of the Hopi Indians of Third Mesa*. Peabody Museum of American Archaeology and Ethnology, Papers, Vol. 22, No. 1, Cambridge, Mass.

TWITCHELL, R. E.
  1912. *Leading Facts of New Mexican History.* Vol. I. The Torch Press, Cedar Rapids, Iowa.
U. S. DEPARTMENT OF THE INTERIOR
  1860–1900. Annual Reports of the Commissioner of Indian Affairs to the Secretary of the
    Interior, Washington, D.C.
  1894. "Moqui Pueblos of Arizona and Pueblos of New Mexico," in *Report on Indians Taxed and
    Indians Not Taxed in the United States at the Eleventh Census: 1890.* Washington, 1894.
  1937. *Constitution and By-Laws of the Hopi Tribe, Arizona.* U. S. Office of Indian Affairs,
    Washington.
  1940. Code of Federal Regulations, Title 25—Indians, Chapter 1. U. S. Office of Indian Affairs,
    Washington.
VICTOR, FRANCES E.
  1871. *The River of the West: Life and Adventure in the Rocky Mountains and Oregon.* Hartford,
    Conn.
VOTH, H. R.
  1901. *The Oraibi Powamu Ceremony.* Field Columbian Museum Publication 61, Anthropological
    Series, Vol. 3, No. 2. Chicago.
WHITE, L. A.
  1932a. "The Acoma Indians," *Forty-seventh Annual Report [for 1929–1930],* Bureau of American
    Ethnology, pp. 17–192. Smithsonian Institution, Washington.
  1932b. *The Pueblo of San Felipe.* Memoirs of the American Anthropological Association, No. 38.
    Menasha, Wis.
  1935. *The Pueblo of Santo Domingo, New Mexico.* Memoirs of the American Anthropological
    Association, No. 43. Menasha, Wis.
WHORF, B. L., AND R. TRAGER
  1937. "The Relationship of Uto-Aztecan and Tanoan," *American Anthropoloigst,* n.s., Vol. 39,
    No. 4, pp. 609–624.
WINSHIP, G. P.
  1896. "The Coronado Expedition, 1540–1542," *Fourteenth Annual Report [for 1892–1893],*
    Bureau of Ethnology, pp. 330–613. Smithsonian Institution, Washington.

CPSIA information can be obtained
at www.ICGtesting.com
Printed in the USA
LVOW01s1207170316
479587LV00016B/485/P